DISCARDED

SIDE GLIMPSES
FROM THE COLONIAL MEETING-HOUSE

BY

WILLIAM ROOT BLISS

DETROIT
Gale Research Company · Book Tower
1970

This is a facsimile reprint of the
1894 edition published in Boston
and New York by Houghton, Mifflin
and Company.

Library of Congress Catalog Card Number 70-140410

To

MRS. ALICE MORSE EARLE

MY FELLOW TRAVELER
ALONG THE BYWAYS AND HEDGES
OF
COLONIAL NEW ENGLAND

*Side glimpses often bring home
richer results than a broad stare*
RUSKIN

THESE side glimpses will disclose to the reader some facts so small that they have not been thought worthy of mention by historians who have looked at colonial New England with a broad stare. But small facts sometimes reveal large pictures of human life; they make the warp and woof of common history, while deeds of armies and of political parties make its selvages. Thorold Rogers, when lecturing at Oxford on the economic interpretation of history, said that every fact is infinitely valuable. He would have us search for the facts of the life of the English people in such sources as town registers, churchwardens' accounts, court journals, church records, obsolete laws, tax lists, old newspapers, account books, diaries, letters, and all kinds of personal manuscripts.

These are the origin of my Glimpses. In offering them I may have no other merit than that of the bellringer on the highway, who calls attention to his wares. Yet perhaps a passer-by will find some things of interest in them.

W. R. B.

GREYSTONES, SHORT HILLS,
    ESSEX COUNTY, NEW JERSEY.

CONTENTS

	PAGE
THE MEETING-HOUSE DEVIL	1
RUM AND SLAVERY	12
THE COMPOSITE PURITAN	29
THE PERSONALITY OF THE MEETING-HOUSE	46
THE SUMMONS TO WORSHIP	69
THE SEATING OF THE PEOPLE	82
THE WRETCHED BOYS	96
THE DISTURBERS OF PUBLIC WORSHIP	105
THE NEIGHBORS OF THE MEETING-HOUSE	120
THE COMEDY AND TRAGEDY OF THE PULPIT	133
THE POOR PARSONS	149
THE NOTORIOUS MINISTERS	178
THE SIMPLE EVANGELIST	206
THE MUSE OF CHORAL SONG	221
THE BIBLE AND THE CONFESSIONAL	234
THE HOUR-GLASS	249

"With innocent necromancy he calls the dead out of their graves, and makes them play their drama over again."

JAMES ANTHONY FROUDE.

SIDE GLIMPSES FROM THE COLONIAL MEETING-HOUSE.

I.

THE MEETING-HOUSE DEVIL.

FOR a hundred and forty-eight years an enormous brass weather-cock whirled on the tip of the steeple of the old brick meeting-house in Hanover Street. There,

> "With head erect, and unruffled form,
>   The hearty and tough old cock,
> Through wind and rain, and cold and warm,
>   All weathers continued to mock;
> And he whisked him round to face the storm
>   And breast himself to the shock."

He was nearly two hundred feet above the street; three times as high as the highest chimney-cap on Copp's Hill; so high that the steeple on which he stood was the most conspicuous object in Boston, and a landmark to seamen coming up the harbor. There was another landmark on the highlands of Truro, — the great hulk of an old meeting-house, whose windows blinked upon the Atlantic Ocean, which, for years before the Highland Light was built, rendered service to mariners when they sighted Cape Cod; and when Nantucket was in her glory, the homeward-bound whaleship, as she neared the harbor, sent a man aloft to get the bearings of the meeting-house steeple. The conspicuousness of such landmarks in other parts of New England is noted by a writer of the last century, who says that the meeting-house in Dudley "stands on a hill which commands a south prospect of extensive farms to the distance of twelve miles;" and from one at Shrewsbury, — "east, west, north, and south, twelve meeting-houses can be seen."

The meeting-house of colonial New England was the centre of the town; distances along the highways were measured from it; milestones directed the way to it. It stood for certain customs, principles, and opinions which were believed to be as immutable as a divine decree. When I turn back, intent to hear the story it can tell, it rises before me on the hilltop as if it were old Kronos watching, through busy days and silent nights, the events of the past; and it seems to say: —

> "I am old, and have seen
> Many things that have been;
> Both quarrel and peace,
> And wane and increase.
> Of ill and of well
> Is the tale I tell."

The colonial town, isolated in its situation, was like a little province living within itself; its parliament was the town meeting, but its ruling influence was the meeting-house, through which, in one way or another, the entire life of the townspeople passed. This influence did not end with the colonial period; it ran so far into the present century that James Russell Lowell said, in one of his published letters, "New England was all meeting-house when I was growing up."

And yet the work of building it encountered obstacles as various as were the notions of men. When Joseph Emerson preached his first sermon at Pepperell, where he was settled in the year 1747 on a yearly salary of "sixty-two pounds ten shillings and thirty six cords of fire wood," he said: "The Devil is a great enemy to building meeting-houses, and to the utmost of his power stirs up the corruptions of the children of God to oppose or obstruct so good a work." Let me mention a few examples of obstruction made by the Devil to whom this minister referred.

When the town meeting of Hadley voted, in the year 1750, to build a meeting-house in "the center of the town," a dispute arose on the question, Where is the centre? The dispute increased to a quarrel which lasted thirteen years; during that period more than fifty town meetings were convened to agree upon a centre, and were adjourned to continue the quarrel, which was finally ended by a lottery. The result of a quarrel begun at Watertown, in the year 1692, was to build two meeting-houses where one only was needed. The hostile feelings that existed for many years between the opposing worshipers compelled the General Court to order the removal of both edifices to other locations; on the principle, as may be supposed, that kennels of fighting dogs should be far from each other. A quaint method was adopted at Harvard town when the people could not agree upon a location for the meeting-house. Every voter laid a stone where he would have the house set; with these conditions, — that there be two heaps of stones only, that the heap having the largest number of stones shall mark the location, and the selectmen shall "inspect the heaps and see that no man lay more than one stone." When the ceremony was ended, it was found that no choice had been made because each heap contained the same number of stones.

In the middle of the last century, a ludicrous result happened to the plans of certain inhabitants of Concord, a town noted for its ecclesiastical quarrels, who wanted to live in peace and enjoy

> "The easeful days, the dreamless nights,
> The homely round of plain delights,
> The calm, the unambitioned mind,
> Which all men seek and few men find."

They obtained liberty from the General Court to be set off and incorporated as a town under the name of Carlisle; and as soon as they undertook to select a site for their meeting-house they began a quarrel about it. Three years later, being as far as ever from that peaceful condition for which they had been looking, they petitioned the Court to be set back to Concord, with all their former privileges; among which was, of course, that of having their own way.

It was a religion of the New Englander to have his own way. He nourished a will which closed on its purpose as a steel trap closes its jaws on a woodchuck. In his philosophy

"Gifts count for nothing ; Will alone is great ;
All things give way before it, soon or late."

Nothing but this will, stirred into action by a disagreement with his neighbors, caused the migration of Thomas Hooker and his company, through a hundred miles of the forest stretching from Boston to the Connecticut River, in the year 1636. The old historian, William Hubbard, says of them : " Some men do not well like, at least cannot well bear, to be opposed in their judgments and notions ; and thence were they not unwilling to remove from under the power as well as out of the bounds of the Massachusetts." And if we trace back the line until we reach John Rogers, he of the "nine small children and one at the breast" (as pictured in the New England Primer), and his fellows who suffered under the rule of Queen Mary, it may be presumed that they were, like Hooker, victims of "a certain choler and obstinate will."[1]

The faculty of provoking a quarrel and of maintaining it by willfulness was hereditary in the race. At Wareham, as recently as the year 1829, there was a quarrel caused by the fact that proprietors and laborers in cotton and iron mills recently established could not obtain seats in the meeting-house, and they wanted the town to build a larger one. A few men settled the quarrel by silently assembling at midnight, pulling down the old meeting-house, and carting away its remains. Such an act gives a new force to the biological law by which living beings tend to repeat their characteristics in their descendants; for I find in the records of Newbury of the year 1713, that Deacon

[1] "Many wise men begin to suspect that the sufferings of the martyrs and confessors in England were not so much due to virtue and love of God's cause as to a certain choler and obstinate will to contradict the magistrate there." — *Father Parsons*, A. D. 1598; letter in *Historical Manuscripts Commission's Report*. London.

Merrill and Deacon Brown were summoned to give reasons for absenting themselves from the communion table, and they answered in all seriousness that their opponents had stolen the meeting-house, "violently pulling it down and carrying it away contrary to our minds and consent."

When a quarrel was unusually prolonged, it was customary for the General Court to send a "viewing committee" to settle it. The decision of this committee was always final; the house must be built on the spot where the committee "set the stake," and a report was required as evidence that this had been done. The following is one of such reports. It is of the year 1747: "To the Hon[ble] Assembly at New Haven These may inform your Hon[rs] that the Prime Society in Woodbury Have set up a Meeting House in the place where the Courts Com[tee] set the stake Have Covered & Inclosed it & for Bigness Strength & Architecture it Does appear Trancendantly Magnificent pr Joseph Minor Society's clerk."

At Goshen, on the hilltops of Connecticut, where the atmosphere of every summer is fragrant with the odor of white clover blossoms, the farmers of 1740 "voted and declared to be necessary" the building of a meeting-house, but they did not venture to ask of each other the question, Where shall we build it? They sent a petition to the General Assembly of the State, praying for a viewing committee to come over and set the stake.

There were other things to be quarreled about besides the location. At Stamford it was the size; whether it shall be thirty-eight feet square, or forty-five feet long and thirty-five feet wide. The records say that the question was left "to the solemn decision of God by a casting of lots; and the solemn ordinance being had, the lot carried it for a square meeting house." In Wallingford the doctrine of Probation caused a quarrel in the church and a secession from it. The seceders began to build a meeting-house eighteen rods distant from their old house, when an injunction to stop the work was supported by the testimony of two women that a minister could be heard preaching at a distance of eighteen rods. In the mean time there was a hand-to-hand fight in the foundation trenches. This was a "spite meetin' house," a name given to many others that were built in New England under similar circumstances.

But some quarrels had a jovial ending, like that at Mendon, in the year 1727. This had lasted three years, when one of the opposing forces began to show signs of weariness. It was captured by a proposition adopted in town meeting " to provide a barrel of rum towards raising the meeting-house." After the raising, some person attempted to cut down a corner post in the frame ; but the town was in such good spirits that it voted not to try " to find out who hath by cutting damnified the meeting-house."

Such quarrels gave birth to anecdotes which have been preserved in the traditions of New England. It is said that John Bulkley, first minister of Colchester, was noted for his worldly wisdom, and for that reason a quarreling church in a neighboring town appealed to him for help. He sent his advice by letter, and at the same time he wrote to a man working on a distant farm. These missives were interchanged, and that which the church received was this : " You will see to the fences that they be high enough and strong ; and you will take particular care that the Old Black Bull don't get in." When this message from the wise parson had been read, there was silence in the meeting-house. At last the reader laid down the letter, and with an air of extreme seriousness he said to the assembled church: "Brethren, this advice is just what we want! We 've neglected our fences; they 're as rotten as punk. That old black bull means the Devil. He has got into our pasture; and the thing for us to do is to drive him out and set up stouter fences!"

II.

RUM AND SLAVERY.

WHEN the quarrels were ended, they began to build the meeting-house, and they made a holiday when they raised its frame. As soon as the frame was up, the townspeople seated themselves upon its sills to enjoy the eating and drinking by which the event was celebrated. It was a very small town if it had not inhabitants enough to cover the sills.

Provision for the celebration was principally rum. The town of Groton, in the year 1754, appointed two deacons, two captains, two lieutenants, one ensign, and one private to superintend a raising, and to provide "one hogshead of Rum one loaf of white Sugar a quarter of a hundred weight of brown Sugar," and food for one hundred men. The town of Harvard, in the year 1733, "voted to provide two barrils of Rum for Raising — one barril of Rum to be West-india and one New England. One hundred weight of brown Sugar, Likewise Eight barrels of Sider And Eight barrels of Bear." At Carver, in the year 1793, the selectmen bought two barrels of rum which, they said, was "Licker sufficient for the spectators." At Framingham, in the year 1795, "one barrel of rum, three barrels of cider and six barrels of beer" were provided for raising the meeting-house.

The people were not inexperienced in preparing mixed drinks with meeting-house liquors. A formula for the mixture was published at Boston in the year 1757, over the initials of Samuel Mather, which has often been quoted: —

> "To purest water sugar must be joined;
> With these the grateful acid is combined;
> When now these three are mixed with care,
> Then added be of spirit a small share;
> And that you may the drink quite perfect see,
> Atop the musky nut must grated be."

An affinity between the rum and the religion of colonial times was exemplified in the license granted to John Vyall to keep a house of entertainment in Boston; he must keep it near the meeting-house of the Second Church, where he offered his "invitation to thirsty sinners" who were going to hear John Mayo or Increase Mather preach.

It was rum that forced the growth of slavery in New England. The business of distilling it from molasses had become, at the end of the seventeenth century, an important factor in all sea commerce. Connecticut prohibited distilling because it made molasses scarce; but the prohibition was stopped when business began to go where rum could be obtained. In the year 1750, there were more than sixty distilleries in Massachusetts and thirty in Rhode Island turning molasses into rum, gallon for gallon. Rum proved to be the best commodity in trading with the southern colonies for tobacco, with Indians for furs, with Newfoundland fishermen for codfish, and with the Guinea coast for slaves. The commerce in rum and slaves — making a circuit from New England to the West India Islands, thence to Africa, thence back to the islands with slaves, thence home with molasses and such negroes as had not been disposed of at the islands — furnished nearly all the money that was annually remitted to pay for merchandise brought from England. The importation of slaves began early. The first arrival at Boston was by the ship Desire, February 26, 1637, bringing negroes, tobacco, and cotton, from Barbados. She had sailed from Boston eleven months before, carrying Indian captives to the Bermudas to be sold as slaves, and thus she became noted as the first New England slave-ship. In time, slaves were brought to Boston and to Newport direct from Africa. Peter Faneuil, to whom Boston is indebted for its Cradle of Liberty, was deep in the business. Thomas Amory, one of the solid men of Boston, was distilling rum and selling slaves to customers in North Carolina; to one of them he writes in the year 1724, saying: "In the fall we expect negroes here direct from Guinea, a vessel having sailed from here and one from Rhode Island." Advertisements of "Just Arrived" negroes may be seen in the Boston "News-Letter" of the years 1726 and 1727:

"To be Sold. A Parcel of Negros Just Arrived, viz. Men, Women, Boys & Girls; they are to be seen at Capt. Nathaniel Jarvis's House near Scarlets Wharff."

"Likely Negro Boy & a Girl just arrived, to be Sold by Mr. Samuel Sleigh, at Messieurs Oliver & Welsteed's Warehouse on the Dock, Boston."

"Several very likely Young Negros of each Sex, just Arrived to be Sold at Six or Twelve Month's Credit, on good security, by Mr. Hugh Hall, Merchant, at whose Ware-house on Mr. Pitt's Wharffe is sold Barbadoes Rum."

There was no hesitation in selling slaves on the auction block. I find in the Boston "News-Letter" of September 19, 1715, a notice of an auction sale "at Newport, R. I., of several Indians, Men and Boys, and a very Likely Negro Man;" and in the issue January 29, 1730, is advertised an auction sale in Boston of "Two Likely Negroes." They were treated in all respects as merchandise; they were rated with horses and cattle. In an inventory of the property of Parson Williams, of Deerfield, of the year 1729, his slaves Mesheck and Kedar were rated with a "one eyed horse" and a "weak back cow" at £80 each. I copy these lines from the inventory of Thomas Bunker's estate, at Nantucket, in the year 1721 : —

"the Indian boy Peleg . . . . £20.—"
"the Indian girl Darcas . . . £10.—"
"an old horse . . . . £ 5.—"
"22 turkeys . . . . £ 2.—"

In an inventory of the estate of Damaris Coffin, of Nantucket, in the year 1728, are three negro slaves rated at £107 10*s*., and two hundred and seventy-four sheep, with ninety-seven lambs, rated at £105 12*s*. In an inventory of her neighbor, Nathaniel Gardner, in the year 1729, I find "one negro boy Toby" rated at £90, with a bull, a cow, a horse, twenty-seven sheep, eleven pewter porringers, a warming-pan, and a clock at £62. Slaves were the most valuable part of the homestead property.

The mother of a slave had no title to her child, as appears from the following advertisements published at Boston, in December, 1726: —

"A Likely Young Negro Woman that hath been about Twelve Months in the Country, and her child Four Years Old, To be Sold."

"There is a strong able Negro Servant Woman of 24 Years of Age fit for either Town or Country Service, being accustomed to both, hath had the Small Pox and speaks good English. As also a Child of 16 months Old. To be Sold."

The Virginian as well as the West Indian plantations were buyers of slaves from New England importers. I find a letter written by William Fitzhugh, of Westmoreland County, Virginia, to "Mr. Jackson, of Piscataway, in New England," dated February 11, 1682, saying: "As to your Proposal about the bringing in Negroes next fall, I have this to offer... to give 3000 lbs Tobacco for every Negro boy or girl that shall be between the age of seven and eleven years old, and to give 4000 lbs Tob. for every youth or girl that shall be between the age of 11 to 15, and to give 5000 lbs Tob. for every young man or woman that shall be above 15 years of age and not exceed 24, the said Negroes to be delivered at my landing some time in Sepr. next."

The money value of a slave in each of these three classes was, at that time, £12, £16, and £20. About the middle of the next century, the money value of a slave of the last class was stated in this bill of sale, by which the seller shows a resemblance to her slave, in the fact that she could not write her own name:—

"Milton June the 9 1747 I the Subscriber Elizabeth Wadsworth of milton have Reced of mr. Timothy Tolman of Stoughton the sum of one Hundred and forty pounds old Tenor in full for a negro fello abought Eighteen years of age named Primas — I say Recd pr me in presence of Benjamin Wadsworth,

her
Elizabeth + Wadsworth "
mark

Sometimes the trade in slaves was kept going at such a brisk gait as to strip the market of rum. In the year 1752, Isaac Freeman wanted a cargo of rum and molasses within five weeks. His correspondent at Newport replied that it could not be had in three months. "There are so many vessels," he said, "loading for Guinea we cant get one hogshead of rum for the Cash. We have been lately to New London and all along the seaport towns in order to purchase molasses, but cant get one hogshead." Captain Scott, not being able to get rum enough to fill his slaver, took dry goods and sailed for Guinea coast. There he found difficulty in exchanging dry goods for negroes, as the wet goods alone were wanted. He wrote home that he had got 129 slaves, of which he had lost 29, and was fearful of losing more. He said: "I have repented a hundred times ye buying of them dry goods. Had we laid out two thousand pound in rum, bread, and flour,

it would purchase more in value than all our
dry goods." Simeon Potter was for watering
the rum and turning it out to the negroes in
short measure. He instructed his captain
sailing for Africa in the year 1768: "Make
your Chief Trade with the Blacks, and Little or none with the white people, if possible
to be avoided. Worter ye Rum as much as
possible and sell as much by short measure
as you can." This man represented the
commercial morality of the times, when honesty was not always considered to be the best
policy. John Hancock was a smuggler of
teas; Peter Faneuil was a smuggler of brandies; it was a common event to find bundles
of shingles short in number, quintals of fish
short in weight, casks of rum and hogsheads
of molasses short in gallons. A punitive
law of the province of Massachusetts Bay,
enacted in the year 1718, and reënacted in
the year 1731, declared that "Hogsheads
and casks which ought to answer the gage
by rod have been proved, and upon tryal in
their drawing off there hath been wanting
seven or eight gallons and sometimes more
in a hogshead which persons are obliged
to pay for." By watering the rum, by

smuggling, by short measures, and by slave-trading, there grew up in the colonial meeting-house a class of rich and respected men, whose descendants have been enjoying results of the wealth so acquired.

At Boston, June 24, 1700, Samuel Sewall — who was known as Judge Sewall, Deacon Sewall, and Captain Sewall, and who preferred the last title to all others — published an anti-slavery tract entitled "The Selling of Joseph." He said: "Having been long and much dissatisfied with the Trade of fetching Negros from Guinea; at last I had a strong Inclination to Write something about it." He was in favor of a law imposing an import tax on slaves; "that all Importers of Negros shall pay 40 shillings per head to discourage the bringing of them." As time passed on and the slave trade flourished, this goodman must have dismissed his anti-slavery opinions; for I have read in the Boston "News-Letter" of June 23, 1726, an advertisement of which I here give a copy: "To be sold by Mr. Samuel Sewall at his House in the Common, Boston, several likely Young Negro Men & Boys Just Arrived."

The business of trading in slaves was not immoral by the estimate of public opinion in colonial times. A deacon of the church in Newport esteemed the slave trade with its rum accessories as home missionary work. It is said that on the first Sunday after the arrival of his slaver he was accustomed to offer thanks "that an overruling Providence had been pleased to bring to this land of freedom another cargo of benighted heathen to enjoy the blessings of a Gospel dispensation."

Rum was not only distilled in the New England colonies, it was also imported from the West Indies to supply an increasing demand. It was advertised for sale with dress goods and articles for women's wear; such advertisements I have seen in Connecticut newspapers of the years 1786 and 1791: —

" St. Croix Rum
By the hogshead very cheap.

Callicoes and Chintzes, Lawns and Cambrics, Black and Green Persians, Modes, Lustrings, Silk and Linen Handkerchiefs, Rattinets, Durants, Tummies, Moreens, Calimancoes, Tamboreens. Jamaica and Antigua Rum By the Hogshead and Barrel."

A merchant advertises that "St. Croix Rum will be given for a few thousands of one and an half inch square-edg'd White Oak Plank, or Red Oak hogshead staves." He is fitting out a vessel for a voyage to the West Indies and Africa. Farmers in the vicinity hearing of his wants carry in their oak planks and staves, and return home loaded with rum. Rum is found afloat as well as ashore. I quote an instance from a Norfolk paper of June, 1787 : —

"On the evening of the 9th the Packet Joseph and Peggy, from New York, bound for this port, was lost on a reef of rocks near Smith Island. The captain, crew, and one woman passenger clung to the shrouds, and in this perilous situation remained until next morning, when they fortunately reached the shore in their boat. On their landing the barbarous and inhuman conduct of ruffians in the form of men surpassed the reception they met with from raging elements, who in place of rendering every assistance in their power, accumulated their distress by plundering what few articles they saved; and at the very time the ocean as it were pitied the sufferings of her victims by floating a couple of barrels of rum, so acceptable at this juncture, the monsters, insensible to every tie of nature or compassion, forcibly seized them, and left these children of misfortune to shift for themselves."

An end of slave trading and a decrease of rum distilling in New England began to appear soon after the constitution of the State of Massachusetts was adopted. In the year 1781, Nathaniel Tennison, a farmer of Barre, who owned ten slaves, was indicted for "assaulting beating and imprisoning" one of them named Quock. He was tried in the Supreme Judicial Court, where his defense that Quock was a slave brought from Africa and sold to him was answered by the Declaration of Rights embodied in the constitution of the State: "All men are born free and equal and have certain natural, essential, and unalienable rights." The court decided that slavery had been abolished in Massachusetts by the adoption of its constitution and Declaration of Rights.

In Connecticut a law of the year 1784 declared that all slaves thereafter born shall be free at twenty-five years of age. But the trade in slaves was continued, as appears from this advertisement in the New Haven "Gazette" of November 9, 1786: —

"To be sold at public vendue on Tuesday the 29th of November instant, at the dwelling house of Captain Enos Atwater, of Cheshire, deceased, a good Negro Wench, about twenty years old. Also a brass wheel'd Clock, a weaver's Loom, with tackling, sundry feather beds, and furniture and a variety of articles of household furniture too numerous to mention."

And this from the New Haven "Chronicle" of January 23, 1787:—

"Wanted to Purchase. A number of likely Young Negroes from 14 to 20 years of Age. Enquire of D. Bowen."

And this from the New Haven "Gazette" of April 19, 1797:—

"To be sold a healthy strong and active Negro Boy, about 11 years of age. Enquire of the printers."

The Connecticut census of the year 1790 showed a slave population of more than two thousand; its fugitive slaves and slaves for sale were advertised up to the end of the century.

In Rhode Island, the legislature enacted that no person who may be born after the first day of March, 1784, shall be held as a slave, and three years later all slave trading in that State was prohibited by laws with severe penalties. But as slavery made a profitable market for rum, the trade was continued between Africa and the West India Islands by Rhode Island men and Rhode Island vessels, which came home to Newport to renew their outfits. A letter dated at Newport, May 9, 1791, and printed in the "American Museum" of that year, says:—

"On the 7th instant arrived here from an African sea voyage (but last from Havannah, where the slaves were sold) a bark belonging to this town commanded by a Captain Wolf, owned by said Wolf and Caleb Gardiner. One that was on board this vessel, during the voyage, informed me that a few days after they sailed from Africa symptoms of the small-pox appeared upon a female slave. She was kept in the maintop three days then taken down, brought to the side of the vessel and thrown overboard by the captain himself. It is said the reason of his drowning her was lest she should communicate the disease to those on board who had not had it."

The universal custom of drinking rum is the saddest fact in the history of the colonies, and it occasionally aroused a protest from the colonial pulpit. James Keith, preaching at Bridgewater in the year 1717, said: "Besides other evils which might be mentioned, I would refer particularly to the excessive and prodigious expense upon strong drink; above all that of Rum; I say the scandalous and horrible abuse of Rum which threatens this land and this place." A specification in Cotton Mather's indictment against the people of New England, which, in his own handwriting, is preserved in the Massachusetts archives, was "A Flood of Excessive Drinking with Incentives thereto." One of these incentives was the general custom of anointing the frame of a meeting-house with rum; and the habits of excessive drinking, thus formed at the meeting-house, ran down to distant generations through the mysterious channels of heredity. Men were often to be seen standing up to confess before the congregation that they had been "overtaken with strong liquor." Rum became as abundant as water; there was no assembly, from a wedding to a funeral, without it. In harvest time the meeting-house bell was rung, at eleven o'clock in the forenoon and at four o'clock in the afternoon, to call laborers from the fields to drink their allowance of rum. Once a year, in sleighing time, farmers drove to Boston or to Newport with their farm products, to be sold; and they always loaded their sleds for the return journey with rum, first; then they took tobacco and salt codfish; then, if there was any money left from the sales, they bought tea and coffee for the women folks.

Two generations ago, intemperate drinking began to disappear; and when a meeting-house frame was raised at Plymouth, Mass., in the year 1831, it was stated as a remarkable fact that "the workmen refrained entirely from the use of ardent spirits." But people who went to sea began to reform themselves earlier than did those who stayed ashore and built meeting-houses. A letter published at Philadelphia the 26th of May, 1791, says: "'T is a fact worthy of notice that no rum or spirit of any kind was used on board the ship Brothers, Captain Josiah, on the late voyage to Canton. The constant drink of the sailors was spruce beer."

III.

THE COMPOSITE PURITAN.

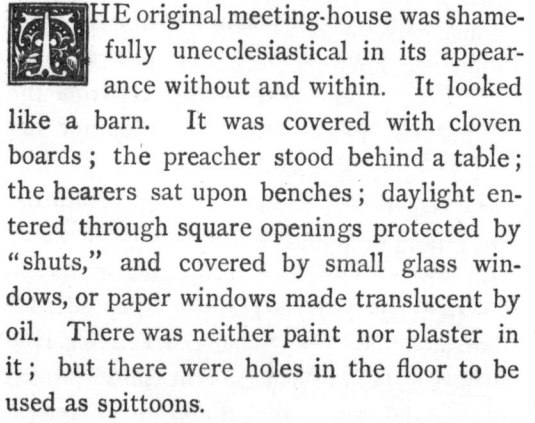

THE original meeting-house was shamefully unecclesiastical in its appearance without and within. It looked like a barn. It was covered with cloven boards; the preacher stood behind a table; the hearers sat upon benches; daylight entered through square openings protected by "shuts," and covered by small glass windows, or paper windows made translucent by oil. There was neither paint nor plaster in it; but there were holes in the floor to be used as spittoons.

Townspeople habitually grumbled when taxes were proposed for making repairs, and therefore the meeting-houses of New England fell gradually into a dilapidated condition; like that in Salem village, which, as say the records of the year 1692, remained "for a great while without any repairs so that by reason of broken windows stopt up by boards and others wide open it is sometimes so cold that it is uncomfortable and sometimes so dark that it is almost unuseful." In this shabby house, built for divine worship, I hear the minister complaining of "the Lord's table not being provided with aught else but two pewter tankards." The Salem meeting-house was not a solitary example. A warrant for a town meeting at Rochester, in the year 1731, said that the object was "To know ye Towns Mind Respecting some speedy care & propper method to Repair the Meeting House so as to make it comfortable to attend ye publicke worship." A warrant for a town meeting at Wareham, in the year 1756, said: "To see if ye Town will raise money enough to Repair the Meeting House Glass Windows and make it comfortable."

Similar had been the state of things in Old England. The "decays of churches and unseemly keeping of chancels" had become so common in rural towns that Ecclesiastical Commissioners, by direction of Queen Elizabeth, ordered the tables of Commandments to be "set up in the east end of the chancel, to be read not only for edification but also to give some comlye ornament

THE COMPOSITE PURITAN. 31

and demonstration that the same is a place of religion and prayer." These tables of the Commandments, which were usually flanked by ornate pictorial representations of Moses and Aaron as large as life, were whitewashed, or were torn down and broken in pieces, by the Puritan zealots who ruled England at times before the Restoration.[1]

There was no authority competent to set up the Commandments or any comely ornament in the colonial meeting-house. Its interior represented the barrenness of the colonial mind. But this was not true of all English colonies; the meeting-house in which the first legislature of Virginia assembled at Jamestown, in the year 1619, had pulpit and pews built of cedar, wide windows that could be opened and shut according to the weather, and its interior was kept "passing sweet and trimmed up with divers flowers." The people who formed the New England colonies, being of a coarser type, had not been taught the love of flowers; they felt no desire

[1] In the Chronicle of the Grey Friars of London, A. D. 1547, days are mentioned when "in dyvers paryche churches alle imagys pullyd downe thorrow alle Ynglonde and all churches new whytte lymed with the commandmenttes wryttyne on the walles."

to adorn their houses of worship with festoons of clematis and honeysuckle and trailing arbutus; nor did they care to preserve them from decay. They were required by law to build a meeting-house, and by various laws they were required to go to worship in it. Such laws were enacted and reënacted from the beginning of the colonies; and in the year 1715 the legislature of Massachusetts declared that all able-bodied persons, "not otherwise necessarily prevented," who "shall for the space of one month together absent themselves from the publick worship," shall be fined twenty shillings; and, if unable to pay the fine, "to be set in the cage or stocks not exceeding three hours according to the discretion of the justices." The existence of these laws is evidence that church-going was not a love of the people; and this fact can be accounted for if you will look at the ingredients composing the population which has been called Puritan.

It was during the reign of Queen Elizabeth that "Puritaine" became a name. The clergy of the Church of England were at a difference in regard to wearing what John Fox called "mathematical caps with four corners," and "theatrical dresses," and "Popish insignia." A royal decree published in March, 1564, made it imperative upon all ministers of the Gospel to wear the regulation vestments when officiating at Divine service. Dissent from this decree by many ministers became so strenuous that the Archbishop told the Queen, in regard to the dissenters, "These precise folks would offer their goods, and their bodies to prison rather than relent." Then the dissenters were first called Puritans; as "men that did profess a greater purity in the worship of God, and a greater detestation of the ceremonies and corruptions of Rome than the rest of their brethren."

The Puritan made himself conspicuous by resisting the impositions of the rubric as to the use of the cross in baptism, the ring in marriage, and the kneeling posture at the communion. He refused to join in religious services under the guidance of a minister wearing a surplice or other vestments of the Church of England. He could say: —

"I am no quaker not at all to sweare,
　　Nor papist to sweare east and mean a west,
　But am a protestant and will declare
　　What I can nott and what I can protest.

"Paul had a cloake and bookes and parchments too,
  But that he wore a Surplice I 'll not sweare,
Nor that his parchments did his orders show,
  Or in his bookes there was a Common prayer." [1]

The opinion of a period is seldom at fault in estimating the character of men and events belonging to it. I may therefore quote from a letter of the " Salvetti Correspondence," dated at London 16th December, 1628, which says of the Puritans: "With those people it is a maxim to oppose everything, never to be satisfied with the present nor to agree with what is proposed for the future."

The New England Puritan was not, like the daughters of Jupiter, "crippled by frequent kneeling." In the services of public worship he would not kneel, but stood up for prayer; would not stand up, but sat down for singing; would not allow the Bible to be read from the pulpit; would not broaden the *a* in Hades; would not have Christmas day nor Easter morning in his calendar.[2] His

[1] From satirical verses of the period of the Restoration.
[2] It was not until the year 1681 that the Massachusetts law forbidding the observance of Christmas Day was repealed. But the Puritan still hated it. We get a savor of his hatred in Sewall's diary of the year 1685, Christmas

climax is seen in the bigotry of John Endicott cutting out the cross of St. George from the flag of his country, because the Cross was a symbol used by the Church of Rome. The religious Puritan to whom the Cross was an offense was a darkened being. There could have been but little of the true devotional spirit in men or women who regarded with aversion that emblem of the Passion which stirs devotional hearts to-day. Not for them was the sentiment of Xavier's hymn : —

>"Tu, tu, mi Jesu, totum me
>Aplexus es in Cruce."

Palfrey says that the Puritan represented the "manliness of England." It is truer to say that he represented the obstinate willfulness of the English race. His ranks contained two distinct classes: the doctrinal and the state Puritans. To secure a political independence, many doctrinals came to New England, leaving a land in which John Milton stood for freedom, to form a state from which Roger Williams could be banished.

Day: "Carts come to town and shops open as usual; some somehow observe ye day, but are vex'd, I believe, that ye Body of ye People profane it; and, blessed be God, no authority yet to compell them to keep it."

It is well known that here they became intolerant and unmerciful, and, as their friend Sir Richard Saltonstall said, did "fyne whip and imprison men for their consciences." They did this not because of the exigencies of their political situation, nor because the teachings of the time were cruel; but because they had a mission which they could carry on only by claiming their own way in all temporal and spiritual matters.

They landed in Massachusetts with intention to establish a "Theocrasie." John Winthrop had thought of it on the voyage, and John Cotton published it in his letter to Lord Say and Sele, in which he said: "Theocracy is the best form of Government in the Commonwealth as well as in the Church." As the Puritan idea was that rigid discipline is necessary for man, and coercion by laws is a necessary part of discipline, they legislated to punish a temper of mind and a fashion of dress, as well as to prevent crimes. They based their laws on a historic covenant with the ancient Hebrews, and they said, "No custom nor prescription shall ever prevail amongst us . . . that can be proved to be morally sinful by the

Word of God."[1] They harassed opponents for nothing which can be acknowledged to have been a crime; and they would have put John Bunyan into Bedford Jail, had Bunyan and Bedford been in Massachusetts or Connecticut. Their scheme of government eventually failed; but they never had any desire to establish one on the principles of civil and religious liberty.

All this is to be accounted for by the fact that they were disciples of John Calvin. Who was he? He was a theologian who lived between the years 1509 and 1564, in France and Switzerland; and was the inventor of a system of theology which for nearly three centuries exercised a prodigious influence upon all persons who accepted it. This system teaches that the only assurance of salvation which a believer in the Christian religion can have rests upon God's sovereign purpose, whereby he has predestinated some men, women, and children to eternal life, and others to eternal death. The fortunate ones are said to be "effectually called," and to be kept in a line of progressive holiness unto

[1] *The General Laws and Liberties of the Massachusetts Colony*, 1648–1672.

the end. Calvin rendered some service to the progress of human thought; but he was as bigoted and intolerant as any man of his time. At his instigation Michael Servetus, a theologian whose orthodoxy he doubted, was arrested, while in church at Geneva, and imprisoned. Calvin desired to have him beheaded; but the civil council condemned him to be burned at the stake; and thus this preacher perished in October, 1553. Calvin then found it necessary for his own justification to publish a treatise, which appeared in February, 1554, entitled a "Defense of the Doctrines of the Trinity against the detestable Errors of Michael Servetus, wherein it is also shown that it is lawful to punish Heritics with the sword." A few weeks later there appeared a "Treatise concerning Heritics," — a collection of passages from various authors in favor of religious toleration. It was compiled by Sébastien Castellion, who in his preface to the book shows the unimportance of such doctrines as Predestination, and sets forth Christianity as a system of life, and not a system of dogma. Michelet says that he established for all time the great law of tolerance ("posa pour tout l'avenir la grande loi de la tolérance"). Calvin had already declared that heretics ought to be punished with death. He knew Castillion; he pursued him with relentless persecution; declared that he was Satan's emissary to deceive the thoughtless; stigmatized him as "blasphemous, malignant, full of animal lusts, a dirty dog, impious, obscene."

John Calvin was duplicated in the Puritans who founded New England. His spirit banished Mrs. Hutchinson and Roger Williams. It hanged the people called Quakers, in the years 1659 and 1660, and the people called witches, in the year 1692. It spoke on the vituperative tongue of Cotton Mather when that subtle priest maligned the men of Boston who established the Brattle Street church, in the year 1700. It burned at the stake a negro slave woman, at Charlestown, in the year 1755; and it tormented the people called Shakers, in the year 1782. The founders of New England are not to be blamed because they were unfriendly to civil and religious liberty, for John Calvin stood behind them and shaped the form and policy of their government.

Plymouth followed in the Puritan train. When Winthrop's company had settled on the peninsula, which, as their records of September, 1630, say, "shalbe called Boston," the Plymouth colony was in a state of decay. It had been ashore nearly ten years, and had not established a town nor created a commerce. So sluggish had been its growth, and so comatose was its condition, that no records of its public life had been written. It had put to death John Billington, one of the London scapegraces who were shuffled aboard the Mayflower while she lay at Southampton, and it had punished others of that class, whose mutinous speeches had caused the self-protecting "compact" to be signed in the cabin of the ship when she was at anchor in Cape Cod harbor. Its trusted agent, Isaac Allerton, had "plaid his own game," as Governor Bradford wrote, "and rane a course to ye great wrong & detrimente of ye plantation;" whose future he said, was "foulded up in obscurite & kepte in ye clouds." Many of the people were dissatisfied with the location; they said the harbor was the poorest and the soil the barrenest on the coast of New England.

While the Massachusetts colony was founding many towns, the Plymouth colony was steadily loosing its population. Winthrop, writing in the year 1646, felt thankful, in his sympathy for the colony, that "one Captain Cromwell," a privateer with three ships and eighty men who had captured richly laden Spanish vessels in the West Indian seas, had been forced by adverse winds into Plymouth harbor; he said, "Divine Providence so directing for the help of that town which was now almost deserted."

The Plymouth colony was saved from ruin by an overflow into it of people from the Bay colony who had the means of living. Erelong it became true that the two colonies were one in theology and politics. As James Cudworth, the magistrate of Scituate, wrote: "Plymouth Saddle is on the Bay horse; our Civil Powers are so exercised in matters of religion and conscience that we have no time to effect anything that tends to the promotion of the civil weal; but must have a State religion and a State ministry and a State way of maintenance."

The population was a peculiar mixture of human beings. At the outset, doctrinal Puritans sent by commercial adventurers and accompanied by educated ministers, who were to convert the Indians, came to the Massachusetts in congregations and in companies. The immigrants who came later were mainly of a different sort. They were not religionists. They came out of a stratum of society lying between the gentry and the peasantry of England. No representatives of science, or art, or literature came; no statesman, no poet came; nor any great leader of social life. But there did come, with a few merchants and lawyers, shiploads of common people moved by the same love of adventure which to-day carries Englishmen to unknown lands : yeomen, tradesmen, mechanics, servants, and idlers. "And by this mean," as Bradford wrote, "the cuntrie became pestered with many unworthy persons."

These all put together made the composite New England Puritan. Into this mass must be mixed Huguenots, Germans, Scotch prisoners sent by Cromwell, and white slaves imported from Ireland to be sold, who became the forebears of a part of the population; and to complete the contents of the cauldron I must add the abundant offspring of miscegenation between the Indian and the white races. Those were licentious times when Winthrop, writing to Plymouth, July 28, 1637, thought it necessary to say, of the captives taken in the Pequot war: "We have ye wife & children of Mononotto, a woman of a very modest countenance and behaviour. It was by her mediation that the English maids were spared from death, and were kindly used by her; so that I have taken charge of her. One of her first requests was that the English would not abuse her body." That Indian mother spoke a better morality than was then prevalent in New England. There is now in existence a manuscript letter concerning the Pequot captives, from Israel Stoughton to Governor Winthrop, which is indorsed by the Governor, "Received 5th month 6th day 1637." It speaks of 48 or 50 women and children taken captives, and then it says: "There is a little squa that Steward Calacot desires to whom he hath given a coate. Lifetenant Davenport also desires one, to witt a tall one that hath three stroakes upon her stummach thus ! ! ! he desireth her if it will stand with your good liking; the Solomon ye Indian desireth a young little squa which I know not, but I leave all to your dispose."

All these people were required by law to sit in the colonial meeting-house. They were nominally Puritans, and are so spoken of by historians and orators. They acquired certain habits of mind under Calvinian teachings which became characteristic of their descendants, in whose acts to-day appears the original composite ancestor.

Many of Miss Wilkins's character stories may be read as true delineations of the composite Puritan's hereditary traits, which are still clinging to the rural New Englander as moss clings to the old stone walls on his farm. For example, there is Marcus Woodman, who said that the minister "was n't doctrinal." He spoke about it in church meeting, and he kept getting more and more set, every word he said. He had a way of saying things over and over, as if he was making steps and raising himself up on them. Finally he said if that minister was settled over that church, he himself would never go inside the door. Somebody replied, "You'll have to sit on the steps, then, brother Woodman." He answered, gritting his teeth, "I will sit on the steps fifty years before I'll go into this house, if that man is settled here!"

There was the doctrinal Puritan! His mind was full of the stubborn animosity of his remote composite ancestor, whose facial features he showed in "a mild forehead, a gently curving mouth, and a terrible chin with a look of strength in it that might have abashed mountains." Sunday after Sunday he walks to the meeting-house with Esther Barney, to whom he is engaged to be married, and takes a seat on the steps while she passes within.

People ask: "Is that Mr. Woodman crazy?"

The answer is: "No; he has got too much will for his common sense, and the will teeters the sense too far into the air."

So it was with the Composite Puritan of New England.

IV.

THE PERSONALITY OF THE MEETING-HOUSE.

THE first refinement made in the colonial meeting-house was the elevation of the preacher into a pulpit. Pulpits were beautiful works of art in the cathedrals of England, and more beautiful in those of Flanders and the Netherlands. But some Puritans and Quakers had condemned them because, as one of the latter said "They have a great deal of superfluity and vain pains of carving, painting, and varnishing upon them, together with your cloth and velvet cushion, because of which, and not for the height of them above ground, we call them Chief Places."

Of the parishes of England it was required that every church shall set up "a comley and honest pulpit, in a convenient place, for the preaching of God's word." The green cushion adorning the pulpit was an object of special interest. A story of the creation of this indispensable ornament is told in a parish record [1] of the year 1635: —

	li.	s.	d.
Pd for foure gras greene taselles for the Cossen .	0	12	0
for Silke for pulpit cussen	0	7	8
for two ounces and halfe of greene fringe .	0	6	3
for halfe yard of greene broadcloth	0	6	6
for 7 pounds of flocks	0	3	6
for 9 yardes of Gould chaine and 3 quarterns	0	6	6
for Satin and four skenes of silk	0	1	10
for one ell of canvis	0	1	5
John Prince for making the Coshen . . .	0	5	0

Church records of Medford state that on Sunday, July 28, 1771, "was used for the first time the new pulpit cushion given by William Pepperell, Esq[re], who imported it from England at a cost of eleven guineas."

In the second century of New England, the pulpit became large and lofty, resembling a section of a fortress; the long stairs ascending to its door were covered with a carpet; a canopy or sounding-board was suspended over it, in which bats made nests; "and it was no uncommon thing," as the Branford annals say, "for a bat to get loose

[1] *The Church Warden's Accounts of the Parish of St. Mary's, Reading, Berks*; 1550 to 1662.

during the service and go scooting through the house." Dorcas made a green velvet cushion for the pulpit; one of the selectmen put on his Sunday clothes and with much ado rode off to Boston to buy an hourglass for it; and at last it became the Chief Place in the colonial meeting-house.

The oak pulpit and the green cushion of a meeting-house which was built at Salem in the year 1713 are mentioned in a private letter of that date, which says: "The meeting-house is well built 3 stories high, 28 by 42 feet, with oak timber and covered with one and one-half inch plank and with clapboards upon that, and it is intended to have ye inside finished with plastering when ye Precinct are able. Ye pulpit and ye deacons seat are made of good oak; and a green cushion on ye pulpit given by Mr. Higginson. I had ye above particulars from Mr. Drake ye builder of ye house who is a man of considerable acquirement. He also told me that he prepared a box to put under ye foundation containing ye year of our Lord that ye building was begun, and various particulars about ye framing of ye church. He also put in copper coins of ye reign of our blessed Sovereign Queen Anne, and an epistle to ye sovereign who shall reign over these Provinces when ye box shall be found, and another to ye Household of faith in Salem Middle Precinct exhorting them to maintain ye doctrine of ye founders, to ye utter confusion and sham of all Baptists Mass mongers and other heretical unbelievers. Mr. Trush who is himself a Godly man and a member of ye church would not agree to put ye box under ye house, as they thought it savored of presumption and vain glorying; and some of them would not agree to ye sentiments of ye letter to ye Household of faith, but he privately put ye box under ye pulpit, when ye house was near built, enclosed in brick and good clay."

In winter the colonial meeting-house was a cold place. It may be said that the congregation sat "shivering on the brink" of perdition, if the icy temperature of the house and the terrible doctrines of the sermon are to be taken together. Samuel Sewall notes that there was a "Great Coughing" in the congregation; that the sacrament bread was frozen as hard as pebbles, and pieces of it rattled as they fell in the pewter plates.

His description of the temperature was true for nearly two hundred years. The winters in New England were colder than they are now. Sewall has mentioned in his diary a wintry Sunday in January, 1716: "An extraordinary Cold Storm of Wind and Snow. Blows much worse on coming home at Noon, and so holds on. Bread was frozen at the Lord's Table. . . . At Six-a-clock my ink freezes so that I can hardly write by a good fire in my Wive's Chamber." Another wintry Sunday is described by Cotton Mather in February, 1717: "On the 24th day of the month comes Pelion upon Ossa; another snow storm came on which almost buried the memory of the former, with a storm so famous that Heaven laid an interdict on the religious assemblies throughout the country, on this Lord's Day, the like whereunto hath never been seen before." Another wintry Sunday is noted by Rowland Thacher, minister at Wareham, in February, 1773: "A remarkably cold Sabbath reaching as far as New York. Some by their glasses found it to be many degrees colder than ever was known in New England. Many were froze. I myself coming home from Meeting had my face touched with the frost." This was Arctic weather; and the obstinacy with which New England congregations sacrificed themselves to it, during two centuries, was piteous. When at last they discovered that it was not sinful to be warm on Sunday, they tried to induce the town meeting to put stoves into the meeting-house. An instance is recorded in the records of Waltham, of the year 1818; some persons of their own volition had set up a stove in the Waltham meeting-house, and had asked the town to furnish fuel for it. They might, says the writer of the story, "as well have applied fire to gunpowder and have expected no explosion." The town ordered the stove to be put out-of-doors. Perez Briggs and Ebenezer Bourne, selectmen of Wareham in the year 1825, called a town meeting, "To see if the Town will furnish sufficient money belonging to the meeting-house to Purchase a Stove and pipes and furnish wood and attendance for said Stove."

What was the town's reply to this request? "Not to purchase a Stove and pipes. Not to furnish wood and attendance. What money belongs to the Town to remain in the Treasurer's hands until otherwise ordered."

Worshipers in these frigid meeting-houses were the people of whom it has been said that they wrote notes of the sermons. The truth was, that the major part of the worshipers could not write, and many could not read. This was true in all parts of rural New England, and it was especially true of women. The popular opinion about girls seems to have been that they were not worth educating; that their natural occupation was servile labor, — to scour the pewter, run the spinning-wheels, wash the dishes and clothing of the family, tend the hens, the geese, and the calves. As late as the year 1785, the town of Northampton voted "not to be at any expense for schooling girls."[1] In regard to men whose days from sunrise to sunset were filled with hard labor, the few who could write were so unskilled in the art that if they had tried to take notes of a ser-

---

[1] In the year 1792, Northampton, after a long struggle in town meeting, voted to admit girls to the town schools from May to October; but those only who were between the ages of 8 and 15 years.

mon the preacher would have reached his "Aymen" long before they had stumbled through his Firstly. It is not to the shame of these people to say that they were illiterate. In the seventeenth and eighteenth centuries that was the general condition of all British communities that tilled the soil for a living. And others beside yeomen were illiterate. This extract from a letter[1] written by Lady Anna Bertie to her friend the Countess of Northampton, in the year 1716, is an example of the illiterate orthography of her class at that time, and their gossip also : —

"I wish this Place afor'd aney thing to make a Letter aney wayes acceptable but all the talke att prasint is of a very od Weding wich has lately happned hear, tho you do not know the Lady I cannot help giveing you an account of, and am Sure did yu know her you must be of my Mind that nothing that weres petticoates need dispair of a husband, She is a boute three score & has nether beauty witte nor good humour to recommend her she is of a make large enough for the Grand Senior. Standing one lucky hour att her

[1] Published by the Historical Manuscripts Commission, London.

Window thear past by a genttellman about the same age who casting hies eyes upwards beheld this Queen of Beauty & att this time was taken with Such a fluttring att his heart that he could not rest till he had Broke his mind to her and he soon found releif, for theay said Matrimony in a week and hethertoo think themselves they happyest Couple in the King's Dominions, God keep them so say I."

The crying want of colonial New England was a school. One of the myths of the colonies, the stock tradition of its histories, is that when a meeting-house was built, a schoolhouse was built also. A historian says: "The schoolhouse and the meeting-house were among the first buildings to be raised in each newly founded village, and as fast as the towns grew to a moderate size these rudimentary schools were supplemented by high schools, and in some instances by Latin schools;"[1] and the latest historian of New England says: "All the early settlers paid great attention to instructing their children first at home, or in the ministers' houses, and then in the public schools, . . . the love of learning never died

[1] John Fiske, lecture at Boston, February 7, 1890.

out, and the free schools were never abandoned."[1]

There is no truth in such general statements. The school history of New England is plainly written in its laws, of which there were a plenty to compel towns to maintain schools ; but they all were "shamefully neglected." A law of Massachusetts which was passed and published June 28, 1702, says : —

"Whereas it is by law appointed that every town within this province, having the number of fifty householders or upwards, shall be constantly provided of a school-master to teach children and youth to read and write; and where any town or towns have the number of one hundred families or householders there shall also be a grammar school set up in every such town, and some discreet person, of good conversation, well instructed in the tongues, procured to keep such school, every such school-master to be suitably encouraged and paid by the inhabitants . . . *the observance of which wholesome and necessary law is shamefully neglected by divers towns*, and the penalty thereof not required."

[1] Douglass Campbell, *The Puritan Holland, England, and America,* pages 30, 31.

The penalty for a non-observance of the school laws was then increased from £10 to £20 yearly; and it was declared that "No minister of any town shall be deemed, held or accepted to be the schoolmaster of such town within the intent of the law." Let me also quote from a Massachusetts law of the year 1718: —

"Whereas notwithstanding the many good and wholesome laws of this province for the encouraging of schools and the penalty first of ten pounds, and afterwards increased to twenty pounds, on such towns as are obliged to have a grammar school master and neglect the same; yet by sad experience it is found that many towns that not only are obliged by law, but are very able to support a grammar school, yet *choose rather to incur and pay the fine or penalty than maintain a grammar school.*"

The penalties were then increased from £30 to £40. These laws tell us what the people thought about schools. They were accustomed to make spasmodic hirings of a schoolmaster, from time to time, in order to show a compliance with the laws; sometimes he was dismissed soon after he was hired; or he was set to work for a few weeks at the centre of the town, a few weeks at an end of it, and a few weeks at the opposite end. In the Wareham records of the year 1756 I read: "And the Select men agreed and Drawd Lotts where the School should begin first, and the first Lot fell to the East End of the Town, the second Lot to the Middle of the Town, ye Third to ye West End." If there was no schoolhouse the teacher taught and boarded in private houses, going from one to another as the shoemaker went on the same circuit to make shoes for the families. When for a long time there had been no school, and the grand jury of the county had "presented the town" for this offense against the laws, the chiefest townsman was sent to answer the presentment, and to get the penalty reduced. These facts are not remarkable if you consider that persons qualified to teach were not numerous, and that money was not plenty in rural towns. The margin of life was so small that it allowed no freedom from labor, and no privilege of being indifferent to the cost of daily necessities.

To return to the meeting-house. As the population and wealth of the colonies increased, the towns began to build meeting-houses of larger size and better quality. These were nearly square, and the roof sloped up from the four sides to a belfry-spire standing on the centre of it. They contained pews; for which long sermons and long prayers must have created a desire. When, for the first time, pews were built in England, it was complained that they were "made high and easie for the parishioners to sleep in;" and the Bishop of Norwich, in the year 1636, found it necessary to direct "that no pews be made over high, so that they which be in them cannot be seen how they behave themselves." A meeting-house built at Newbury in the year 1700 had twenty high and square pews; on the outside of the pews were seats for children; its interior was open to the roof beams, which were polished and ornamented with pendants of a quaint fashion. Then the style was changed to an oblong house with a tower built on one end of it, from which arose a steeple. The Cape Ann meeting-house of the year 1739 was ninety feet long and sixty feet wide; the tower was seventy feet high, and the white steeple, rising seventy feet above the bell-deck, was visible to seamen miles away at sea;

> "Whence sometimes, when the wind was light
> And dull the thunder of the beach,
> They heard the bells of morn and night
> Swing, miles away, their silver speech."

As the style of the colonial meeting-house was changed for the better, so was the dress of the audience changed. In seaport towns a trade with Europe had been established, and the meeting-house felt its influences in the rustlings of silks and ribbons. Broadcloth coats in crimson, yellow, and other colors, began to take the place of dingy homespuns; breeches of buckskin were discarded for breeches of velvet or corduroy; silk camblet hoods, faced with velvet,[1] took the place of cheaper headdresses, and the minister was furnished with a Geneva gown of silk. When reading the manuscript records of a town on Buzzard's Bay, I came upon this, written in the year 1767: "Paid for Doing ye meeting house and for a Sup-

[1] "On the Sabbath, the 28th of Aug last was taken away or Stole out of a Pew at the Old North Meeting House, A Cinnamon Colour'd Womans Silk Camblet Riding-Hood, the head faced with black Velvet." — Advertisement in Boston *News-Letter*, September, 1726.

polidge." The illiterate town clerk probably had in mind a surplice when he invented the word "suppolidge" to signify a Geneva gown, bought for the minister by the town in the time of a general renovation or "doing" of the meeting-house.[1] Mrs. Gamp was inclined to a similar perversion of words: "Mrs. Harris, I says, leave the bottle on the chimney piece, and don't ask me to take none, but let me put it to my lips when so dispoged."

There was no object which the people saw so often as the great door of the meeting-house. Side doors and back doors and private doors it had, but the great door faced the country road on which all travelers passed and tavern-goers loitered. The stepping-stones and the horse-house and the hitching-posts were near it. Every worshiper who approached the meeting-house on Sunday or on lecture day looked at the great door, even if he did not enter thereby. It naturally became the town's bulletin-board

[1] Injunctions issued by Queen Elizabeth directed the parish to pay for the minister's surplice: "Every Minister saying any publick prayers or ministering the Sacraments or other Rites of the Church, shall wear a comely Surplice with sleeves, to be provided at the charges of the Parish."

upon which all informations were posted. The most important of these were the official warnings for a town meeting. When townsmen were unable to read them it became necessary to send abroad the constables to give notice "by word of mouth." This happened at Plymouth, where, as say the records of the year 1694, "the Town declared themselves to be against Warning town meetings by papers set up for that end, but doe Expect warning from the Cunstables by word of mouth when Ever there shall be ocasion."

Other things were also posted on the great door during the first century of New England. Ipswich town compelled the man who hunted wolves, expecting to get the bounty of ten shillings for each wolf killed, to prove his hunt by bringing the heads to the meeting-house and there "nayle them and give notis to the constable." At Portsmouth, it was ordered that the heads must be nailed "upon the meeting-house door;" but at Hampton, near Portsmouth, there was an order that wolf-heads are to be nailed "to a little read oke tree at the north east end of the meeting-hous." Probably the face of the great door was already full of them.

The custom of nailing to the door various things for public warning or knowledge came, like other meeting-house customs of colonial times, from Old England. Many years ago, some fragments of skin were found under nailheads on the principal door of an ancient church in Yorkshire. There was a tradition in the parish that, about a thousand years ago, the church was plundered by a Danish robber; that the robber was captured, condemned to be flayed, and his skin to be nailed to the church door as a terror to evil-doers.[1] During the succeeding centuries the robber's skin, stretched and dried and wrinkled on the door, was wasted away until the only traces of it remaining were small pieces peeping out from under some of the broad-headed nails with which the face of the door was studded. One of these pieces was subjected to the scrutiny of a microscope. Fine hairs were found upon it, — such hairs as grow upon the human body; and the microscope re-

[1] This fact is mentioned in Gosse's *Evenings with the Microscope*.

vealed the fact that they were the hairs of a person of a fair complexion. Thus the general tradition, preserved in the parish for centuries, was shown to be the truth. The fragment taken from the church door was a piece of the skin of a Danish robber, nailed thereon a thousand years ago.

People were as eager to get out of the meeting-house as the colony laws were to get them into it. "There is much profaneness amongst us," say the Massachusetts colony records of the year 1675, "in persons turning their backs upon the public worship before it is finished and the blessing pronounced." The scene described by the formal words of these records was nothing less than a general flight of people from the meeting-house to the open air, as soon as the sermon was ended. It seems to represent the culmination of an agony; like that which is revealed by a hill, in the wild region of Mashonaland, on whose rock are imprinted many footsteps of men and animals, all pointing to the summit, towards which, in some primeval time, they were evidently fleeing in terror from a rising flood. To put a stop to this profaneness, all selectmen were commanded by the General Court to appoint men to bolt or shut the doors of the meeting-house when the sermon was finished, or to act in "any other meet way" to keep the audience inside "until the exercise be ended." Sometimes constables were stationed outside the doors to arrest those who escaped too soon. As the profaneness increased, in spite of the Court, every generation of selectmen was compelled to consider some new "meet way" to stop the stampedes. At last they made rules and regulations directing the manner in which congregations must go out. Here is a regulation put in force at Groton in the year 1756: "After the blessing is pronounced, pews and all the fore seats move out first ; second seats to follow, and so on until the whole house be emptied ; and all persons are to quit the doors as soon as they are out."

As colonial laws empowered selectmen "to order the affaires of the towne," their duties included a care of the meeting-house as well as of roads, fences, and stray cattle. They were such lords of the manor that they, at times, compelled the improvident and the infirm "to voyde the towne." For example, in the year 1701 they gave "notis to a leame gearle whose name is Wodekins," staying at Edward Cooke's house, "that she doe depart out of Dedham." They granted various privileges in the meeting-house, such as to build pews on the overhead beams and in other queer places; as at Rochester, in the year 1718, "to William Blackmer & Timothy Ruggles liberty to build two Seats or Pews six foot fronting from the wall on the beams over the galeries on the East and West Ends of the meeting-house on their own cost;" "to Israel Bumpus & Joseph Haskoll liberty to build a seat all along before the front gallery on their own cost provided they do it decently." They gave privileges "to make glass windows for the conveniency" of pew owners (Pepperell, 1742); to make a private door "from the outside of the meeting-house" (Medford, 1736). This last-named privilege converted the pew to a private box; and I can imagine how eagerly the eyes of homespun gallants watched for the opening of that door, on Sunday mornings, when the belle of the village stepped fluttering in, surprising the deacons by the gravity of her demeanor. In the meeting-house recently built at Crathie, near Balmoral, in Scotland, overlooking a long stretch of the valley of the Dee, a private door was made for the use of her Majesty Queen Victoria, — a convenience similar to that enjoyed by the belle of the colonial village.

The colonial meeting-house was not a consecrated building; for the truth taught at the Well of Samaria was that no place of worship has a distinctive claim of its own. Yet selectmen were called upon to prevent the doing of various things in it; such as, at Hampton, riding horses into it, and firing off guns in it; such as, at Dedham, hitching horses to "the meeting-house Ladder;" such as, at Framingham, "cutting off seats and cutting Holes through the Walls;" such as, at Groton, chewing or smoking tobacco or leaving "any trash in the meeting-house." In its loft selectmen stored the town's gunpowder. There was a little town in Maine whose gunpowder was stored in "the small closets within the sacred desk." On the morning of the battle of Lexington, Captain Parker said to his company: "Every man of you who is equipped, follow me!

And those who are not equipped, go into the meeting-house and furnish yourselves from the magazine and immediately join the company!"

The townspeople were accustomed to assemble in the meeting-house for any purpose of a public nature. But if persons who were not of the orthodox elect desired to assemble therein, they must obtain permission from the town; as at Branford, in the year 1750, the records say that liberty was granted "to professors of the Church of England in this town, as they call themselves, to meet in the Meeting House on they 25th of December which they call Christmas." What a doleful Christmas they found in that Puritan meeting-house! In it ecclesiastical councils sat; and town meetings, always opened by a prayer, were convened, at which men sat with their hats on and made as many disorders as they had a mind to. These were noticed by colony laws and by town laws; such as, "every man shall speak by turn, rising and putting off his hat," and when he has said his say "he shall signify it by putting on his hat and sitting down;" he "shall speak his mind meekly and without noise;" if he "presume to speak without liberty of the moderator," he is to be fined twenty shillings. Notwithstanding these laws of restraint, the walls of the meeting-house resounded at times with a deafening uproar.

> "The constable to every prater
> Bawl'd out — 'Pray hear the Moderator!'
> Some call'd the vote, and some in turn
> Were screaming high — 'Adjourn! Adjourn!'"

V.

THE SUMMONS TO WORSHIP.

THE bells in the tower of Elstow Church were rung by John Bunyan while he was carrying on his trade as the village tinker. The ringing of the bells was a pleasurable diversion from his labors at the forge, because he loved to hear their sounds. This love clung to him through life, and it prompted him to cause all the bells to welcome the pilgrims of his immortal allegory when they entered the celestial city; then "all the bells of the city rang again for joy." When his conscience came under conviction in regard to religious matters he gave up the joyful diversion of bell-ringing, as he gave up that of dancing. Austerity was a religious fashion of his people.

Yet there was a daily ringing of bells in the rural parishes of England. I read in churchwardens' accounts of payments made for the ringing of bells on coronation days, royal birthdays, thanksgiving days, visitation days, wedding days, Christmas days, on many holidays, and whenever a member of the reigning family rode through the town. Then I read of the passing bell, tolled for those who were passing out of this life; and the pealing bell to announce that some mortal had put on immortality. These signified an old belief that devils troubled the dying and lay in wait to afflict the escaping soul, and that they were terrified from their purposes by the bells.[1] After the Reformation that ancient belief in the personal presence and power of devils continued to exist; even Martin Luther, at midnight, heard a devil (and not a rat) cracking nuts near his bedstead. But the reformers taught that the

---

[1] Anno Domini, 1592. (*The Church Warden's Account of the Parish of St. Mary's, Reading, Berks;* 1550 to 1662.)

Rec^d for the passinge Belle for Mr Webbs . . .	4 *d.*
" for the passinge Belle for goodwife Bull . .	4 *d.*
" for the passinge Belle for a stranger diinge at Bonabies	4 *d.*
" for a Prysoners grave and Bell	5 *s.*
" for the double Knill of M^{ris} Elizabeth Busbey and hir child	7 *s.*
" for hir sollome Knill after the Buriall . .	2 *s.* 6 *d.*

passing bell was rung to admonish the living and invite them to pray for the dying.

I read of the prisoner's bell, of the solemn knell after burial, and the double knell for a mother and her child; also of the curfew bell, a signal for all people to cover their fires and go to bed, which was rung from every church spire of England, at eight o'clock of every evening of the year, —

"Swinging slow, with solemn roar;"

and I copy a reference to it from the parish records of St. Mary's in Reading of the year 1600: "that Will'm Marshall the Clarke and Sexten shall have iiij*s.* iiij*d.* a yere more paied him to his wages, and for the same hee is to Ringe the eight a clocke Bell everie evninge both holie daie and workinge daie thoroughe out the whole yere." In the booming life of the present day, when men must drive furiously, or be run over by the throng, one may feel an envy for the peaceful lot of those simpler men and women who lived under the curfew bell.

The villagers of Old England were proud of their bells, and the poorest borough was stimulated to build new bell towers or to hang new chimes. The inhabitants of Totnes in Devonshire were so poor that, in the year 1449, there were only three people in the town who paid as much as twenty pence on "the tax of half-tenths and fifteenths for the King;" and yet the parish determined to replace its wooden belfry by a stone tower, according to the best model, and to rehang its chime of four bells. This was accomplished by coöperative labor of the parishioners, and by contributions of money on Sundays.[1]

In the beginning of New England there were no towns so poor as Totnes. Of but few of them could it be said: —

"Oft in the woodland, far away,
Is heard the sound of bells rung faintly."

The call to worship in most of them was sounded on a drum, beaten back and forth the highway from the minister's house to the ends of the village. Sometimes the sound of a drum was preferred to the sound of a bell; as at Wethersfield, the oldest settlement in Connecticut, the rude forefathers of the hamlet voted "that the bell be rung noe more on the Sabbath or lecture daies,

[1] Green, *Town Life of the Fifteenth Century.*

but the drum henceforth be beaten." The first meeting-house bell in New England was set up in the year 1632 at Newtowne, now Cambridge, on the Charles River. It was a small, shrill-voiced crier, and the people, after hearing its din for four years, became tired of it and used a drum to announce the hour for worship. The first bell at Hingham was so small that when the second house was built, the selectmen were requested to get a new bell "as big againe as the old one was, if it may be had." The first bell at Woburn was set upon a hill back of the meeting-house, to give it a wide hearing. The first bell at Ipswich was hung "on a pine tree to the northeast" of the meeting-house; and the first bell at Malden was set up on a rock which is known to this day as Bell Rock. Near its site is the Bell Rock cemetery, in which graves were made more than two hundred years ago; and near by is the Bell Rock station of a railroad that goes to Boston. Throngs of travelers, hurrying by short cuts across the cemetery to catch the morning trains, have trodden hard paths over the graves of colonial people who came to meeting when they heard the summons from the bell that stood on the rock.

In the year 1659, a bell was hung at Newton; and the records say that John Chamberlin was to have fifty shillings a year for ringing it, and three pounds if he would also keep the meeting-house "doore howlted." A bell is mentioned at Plymouth in the records of the year 1679, when "The Constable is ordered by the Towne to take Course for the sweeping of the meeting house and the Ringing of the bell and to pay an Indian for the killing A woulfe." When a bell was set up at Newbury, the record says that the selectmen procured "a flag for the meeting-house, to be put out at the ringing of the first bell, and taken in when the last bell is rung." In the year 1706, a new bell, "of about four hundred pounds weight," was hung on the meeting-house of this village, and it became a custom to notify the villagers of the flight of time by tolling the day of the month every night after the ringing for nine o'clock. Upon this bell were inscribed the words, "Let us love as brethren!" — a sounding satire on the bitter quarrels which existed for years between the people and their minister.

The bell at Lexington, which was hung in a tower near the meeting-house of the year 1702, must be considered the most famous of all the bells of New England, for on the morning of the nineteenth day of April, 1775, it sounded the first national alarm. It was the original "liberty bell," whose cry went afar on that morning when the embattled farmers "fired the shot heard round the world." Sylvanus Wood, of Woburn, aged seventy-four years, testified, June 17, 1826, "that about an hour before the break of day, on said morning, I heard the Lexington bell ring, and, fearing there was difficulty, I immediately arose, took my gun, and, with Robert Douglass, went in haste to Lexington, which was about three miles distant." This historic bell disappeared in the year 1794, when the old meeting-house was pulled down.

Although there was a bell at Springfield as early as the year 1646, each family was taxed a peck of corn or fourpence in wampum yearly, to pay John Matthews to beat a drum from the minister's house to the end of the settlement every morning and at meeting-time. At Dedham, twenty shillings a year "in cedar boards" were paid to Ralph Day for a similar service. At Haverhill, in the year 1650, Abraham Tyler was chosen "to blow his horn half an hour before meeting;" for which service he was paid with one pound of pork annually from each family. Jedediah Strong, at Northampton, earned eighteen shillings in the year 1679 by "blowing the trumpet" to call people to meeting; at South Hadley, a shell was blown; at Sunderland, a shell, a flag, and a drum were used alternately until the year 1751.

Everybody was expected to go to meeting when the summons was sounded. So ambitious was the real New Englander "to get on in the world" by his own thrift, that he was willing to let his horse on Sunday to those who must ride, while he and his family trudged the way afoot. In a farmer's account book I read, under date of 1737:—

"Samuel Bates D^r for Riding my mare to meeting two days 5 shillings."

"Ebenezer Bates D^r for my mare for your wife to ride to meeting 2 shillings 6 pence."

For a similar reason he rented a part of his pew. The same account book says:

"Daniel Raymond D^r for A right for himself and wife and child in my pue in the meeting hous for one year and half £1-10." This charge was paid with " 2 ounces of Inedeco, 2 gallons of rum, 4 pounds of Shuger and one ounc of peper."

Going to meeting in the summer time was a pleasant tramp for the wayfarer if he had eyes tỏ see the boulders covered with mosses and green tendrils, the roadside trees festooned with grapevines, the creeks skirted with marshmallows, the sandy hillocks clothed in a regal array of foxgloves which nodded to him as he passed by. But in cold and tedious winters the journey was laborious. John Eliot wrote in the Roxbury Church records of the year 1699, "This winter was very sharp and tedious, we had much snow and cold weather, the wayes so difficult and unpassable." Now and then came days in the end of the year when windows were opened, grass was green along the south edges of stone walls, field brooks were running full, and the voice of the mosquito was heard in the land. January shifts the scenes. There arrives a quiet, biting cold; suddenly a whirling snowstorm howls out of the northwest or the northeast, and the highways are speedily covered under deep snowdrifts. From that time all paths to the meeting-house are difficult to be traveled until the sun comes into the north, and alders begin to bloom, and the tips of elms to flush with rosy blossoms, and birds are singing their pertest songs, and foxes have come out of their holes to sit on sunny spots, with ears erect, as if watching the return of spring. But the rustic New Englander, when he trudged to meeting, saw none of these things. He was a man of raw material, burdened with the cares and labors of a frontier life; and never had his eyes been open to the beauty of colors and forms. In this respect his refined posterity is not unlike him; for how many now have eyes to see the lights and shades of nature, or even the lights and shades of the men and women who touch their daily lives?

Riding to the meeting-house of a Sunday, the farmer carries his wife on a pillion behind him, and a child on the saddle in front of him. He rides half the distance and walks the remaining half, leaving the horse hitched to a tree for the use of a part of his family which has followed him afoot; carrying in hand their shoes and stockings, if it is summer, to be put on when they reach the meeting-house. The ways are rough and narrow, following trails which deer have made from the feeding to the watering places. In the year 1685, the Plymouth court was petitioned by seven families of the town of Bridgewater for "a way" to the meeting-house. They complained thus: "God, by his Providence, hath placed the bounds of our habitation in Bridgewater, and on the eastward side of the town, and about two miles from the meeting-house and the mill, and some of us have had no way into the town but upon sufferance through men's lands. We think it is very hard that living in a wilderness we cannot have convenient room for highways."

A love for divine worship may have lightened the steps of many of those who journeyed over the rough ways; but the law compelled them to go even if that love did not exist, and this compulsion created a general habit of going to meeting. While some went to worship in sincerity, others went by force of custom, others to show their finery, to hear the news, to make a trade, to meet their friends, or to satisfy the conscience. Southey tells of a woman in humble life who, going home from the Sunday service, was asked if she had understood the sermon. "Wud I hae the presumption?" was her reply. The quality of the sermon signified nothing to her if she had done her duty in listening to it.

And the minister, as he walked homeward with one of his hearers, said to him: "Sunday must be a blessed day of rest to you who are working hard all the week?"

"Ay, sir!" the man replied. "I works hard enough all the week, and then I comes to church o' Sundays and sets me down, and lays my legs up, and thinks o' nothin'." He was like Tennyson's "Northern Farmer," who "hallus comed to 's choorch" to hear the parson, albeit —

"I niver knaw'd what a meän'd, but I thowt a 'ad summut to saäy,
An' I thowt a said what a owt to 'a said, an' I comed awaäy."

So the Sunday religion of many people can be but little more than a habit of rest for body and mind. Many church-goers there are to-day who have neither the power nor the disposition to turn their thoughts to the subject of which the preacher is preaching; they feel that they are doing their whole duty by giving their presence to the services of worship. Jane Taylor said: —

> "Though man a thinking being is defined,
> Few use the great prerogative of mind.
> How few think justly; of the thinking few
> How many never think, who think they do."

VI.

THE SEATING OF THE PEOPLE.

YOUNG men and young women living far from each other in the same town, working hard all day long during six days of the week, were naturally glad to see each other on Sunday in the meeting-house. But in the arrangement of sittings men were isolated from women. There were "men's seats" and "women's seats," separated by impassable barriers. "No woman maid nor gal shall sit in the mens south alley" was a law of Redding, and it was the determination on which similar laws were made in other towns. At Medford, there was built in the meeting-house a "foregallery" having in it three ranges of seats divided by a barrier athwart them. On one side of this barrier men were placed, on the other side women; and yet there was no authority that could prevent them from viewing each other askance. Two years later, the town voted every "woman maid and gal" out of these seats. The persecuted race rebelled, caused a special town meeting to be convened, and lobbied through an order restoring them to their places.

> "They've beaux to conquer, belles to rival;
> To make them serious were uncivil.
> For, like the preacher, they each Sunday
> Must do their whole week's work in one day."

This unnatural separation of men from women, which may at first have been a precautionary measure, became at last a permanent custom; polished down by rules and regulations until it reached that point where it was assumed to be, as it was called, "a dignifying of the meeting-house." There had been a similar custom in Old England. It is on record that seats in the church at Hawstead were a cause of contentions as early as the year 1287; and the Synod of Exeter tried to abate them by declaring that all persons except noblemen and patrons when they come to church to say their prayers "might do it in what place they pleased." The author of the "History and Antiquities of Hawstead and Hardwick" says:—

"From a decaying paper some years ago in the church chest it appeared that Richard Pead, Reg'rar'ras, directed an instrument to the Church Wardens charging and commanding them to place the inhabitants in such seats in the church as they should think proper, according to their estates, degrees, and callings. Returns were to be made of those that were refractory. Dated, December 1st 1623."

The white people of colonial New England were equal before the law, but unequal before the pulpit; there they were "classed and ranked," as described by Whittier in "Mary Garvin:"—

"When the horn, on Sabbath morning, through the still and frosty air,
From Spurwink, Pool, and Black Point, called to sermon and to prayer,

"To the goodly house of worship, where, in order due and fit,
As by public vote directed, classed and ranked the people sit;

"Mistress first and goodwife after, clerkly squire before the clown,
From the brave coat lace-embroidered, to the gray frock, shading down."

There were no "noblemen and patrons"

waiting to say their prayers in the colonial meeting-house, but there were men of titles who desired to get the best seats in it. "Rank in Our way is Looked upon as a Sacred Thing," said General John Winslow in his letter to the President of Harvard College, October 20, 1740. Therefore military dignity claimed a front seat. There was a good deal of it belonging to officers of militia, and to men who had been in the Indian wars, in the expeditions to Louisburg, Quebec, and Cuba, and who had returned with large stories and small titles. The majority of these were sergeants and ensigns. Even a drummer was somebody in the social scale. "Drummer Stetson" is mentioned in the Scituate records of the year 1725 as an important man. The town of Newbury voted (1700) that "the worshipful Colonel Daniel Pierce should have the first choice for a pew, and Major Thomas Noyes shall have the second choice." Gloucester voted (1742) "that Captain William Haskell should sit in the fore-seat;" and (1757) probably to make room for another captain, "that Mister Joseph Hibbard's wife move out of the long fore-seat into the short fore-seat." At Wallingford (1716), one captain was designated "to set in the deacon's seat," another captain "to set in the first pue," and another "to set in the second pue."

The people made very low bows to an officer of the King, and gave to him a seat of extra dignity. At Norwalk (1686), it was voted: "Thomas Fitch for to be seated in the meeting-house in the upper great round seat, as he is the King's commissioner." His son was assigned to a seat "in the pue with the Justices," and the selectmen desired that he would be so gracious as to "read the psalm and set the tune in the time of public worship." (1723.)

Rules for seating the congregation were not the same in all towns. In some, as at Bedford (1730), the rule was "to have respect to them that are fifty years old and upwards." In others, as at Rehoboth (1718), it was "firstly to have regard to dignity of person, and secondly to age, and thirdly what charge they have been at in building the meeting house;" or, "to have respect to age, office, and estate, negroes excepted." At Harvard (1766), those men who paid the largest taxes had the best seats. The rules were: "The two foremost Seats to be seated by age and pay; the rest of the Seats to be seated by pay only, counting three years back." At Northampton, men were seated in the southwest end and women in the northeast end of the meeting-house. In the year 1737, this town forbade "men and their wives"* to be placed side by side unless "they incline to sit together;" from which I infer that there was not much connubial bliss in Northampton. Judge Sewall appears to have had difficulty in getting his wife permanently seated in the Old South meeting-house. He wrote in his diary, "Lords Day April 1. Sat with my wife in her Pue. April 8, introduced her into my Pue and sat with her there. April 15, conducted my wife to the Fore Seat."

A rule for seating, observed in many towns, was characteristic of the natural itching of the colonists for rank; placing people who had a pedigree and an office at the head, and useful people at the foot of the line: "1st, dignity of descent; 2d, place of public trust; 3d, pious disposition and behaviour; 4th, estate; 5th, peculiar serviceableness of any kind."

Where age was ranked first, wealth was made an equivalent to it. An estate taxed at fifteen pounds, for example, would be declared equal to one additional year in the owner's age. Thus, a person thirty years old, and taxed for three hundred pounds, could add twenty years to age, in his rank, and claim a seat in the meeting-house with those who were fifty years old. But wealth frequently took the precedence of age. At Waterbury (1719), it was voted "to seat by list of estate and by age." At Woburn (1710), the front seats were given to the "wealthy and liberal," and the rear seats to the "aged and poor." The latter complained to the selectmen that they were "much aggrieved at the disorderly seating of many persons in the house of God, the aintient behind the backs of the youth." But the complaint received no attention.

Men who were honored with a seat at a table enjoyed ease as well as dignity. The Framingham records of the year 1701 state that a pew was built "for those men's wives that sit at the table in the north corner of the meeting house." In the year 1715, this town declared "that, as for the dignity of the seats, the table and the fore-seat are accounted to be the two highest; the front gallery is equal in dignity to the second and third seats in the body of the meeting house, and the side gallery is equal to the fourth and fifth seats."

The town of Windsor in Connecticut used an idiom of the present day when, in the year 1717, it expressed its opinion on the subject in these words: "Those that have seats of their own are not to be seated nowhere else." People "hard o' hearin'" were of course destitute of dignity; but they were permitted to sit on the pulpit stairs, or near by, if there was a vacant place, "for the advantage and benefit of hearing the word preached" (Norwalk, 1702), or rather trying to hear it. Old people were also provided for; as at Rochester, in the year 1717, it was "Voted that three Short Seats be built nye the pulpit Stairs for Antiant parsons to sett in."

All were required to occupy the seats assigned to them in the meeting-house, and they were forbidden, as in the parish churches of England, "to press into the seats of others."[1] To enforce these rules a supplement to the Fourth Commandment was adopted, by which it was declared that to sit in the wrong seat "is an act whereby the Sabbath is profaned." When dignities increased so fast that there were not seats enough for those who had equal rank, additional seats were consecrated by a vote of the town, and, on the next Sunday, these new seats were solemnly announced from the pulpit. In "dignifying the meeting-house," white people showed how strong were their antipathies to black people. Negro slaves were placed in the furthermost corners of the galleries, and sometimes in pens on the walls above the galleries. In the Northampton meeting-house, pews were built for negroes near the gallery doors; those for men were labeled B M,

[1] "That whosoever hereafter shallbe Removid by the Churche Wardens from theire Seates to anie other, And heé or thaie beinge so Removid will not tarrie and Abyde in the said Seat but Will or Doe come Backe again, shall paie for everie time so Doinge to the Churche Wardens Twelve Pence, And if it be a woman wch hathe a husband That shall so Offende, Then her husband to paie xij*d* for her, And it be a widowe then shee to paie xij*d* for herselfe." — *St. Mary's, Reading, Berks;* 1550 to 1662.

THE SEATING OF THE PEOPLE.

those for women B W. Jacob Prince, a slave emancipated by the laws of Connecticut, was admitted as a member of the church at Goshen, in "ye yere of owr Lorde god" 1801. He was placed in a gallery pew whose front was boarded up so high that he could not see the congregation from his seat; and, being offended because he was not treated as a "christian brother" in this dignifying of the meeting-house, he at last refused to go to meeting. For this disorder he was excommunicated. Phillis Wheatley, a negro slave who lives in colonial history, sat in the colonial meeting-house, and she dignified it more than some of her white neighbors. She was the author of a volume of "Poems on Various Subjects Religious and Moral," printed in London in the year 1773, on the title-page of which she is described as "Negro Servant to Mr John Wheatley of Boston in New England." She was brought from Africa in the year 1761, when about eight years old; and she expressed her thoughts concerning the transfer in the following lines: —

"'T was mercy brought me from my Pagan land,
Taught my benighted soul to understand

That there's a God, that there's a Saviour too;
Once I redemption neither sought nor knew.
Some view our fable race with scornful eye,
'Their colour is a diabolic die.'
Remember, Christians, Negros, black as Cain,
May be refin'd, and join th' angelic train."

It appears that no general effort was made to convert slaves, lest their conversion might entitle them to personal freedom. In the year 1696, ministers at Boston proposed to the General Court, "That ye wel-knowne Discouragem^t upon ye endeavours of masters to Christianize their slaves, may be removed by a Law which may take away all pretext to Release from just servitude, by receiving of Baptisme." This proposal was not noticed.

Indians also formed a part of the dignity of the meeting-house. They were cribbed with negroes, — and the odor of neither Indians nor negroes was that of sanctity; for in the Plymouth town records of the year 1715, it is written that "the owners of the seat before the place where the Negroes and Indians sett at the meeting house Doe give 3 pounds Towards Erecting a plase for said Negroes and Indians to sett in Elsewhere." The Indians were captives of war who had been sold into slavery. At a Bridgewater town meeting of the year 1676, "a vote was called to see what should be done with the money that was made of the Indians that were sold last, and it was voted that the soldiers that took them should have it." Cotton Mather wrote in one of his diaries, "I bought a Spanish Indian and bestowed him as a servant on my father." John Bacon, of Barnstable, directed in his will that his Indian slave Dinah be sold and proceeds "improved by my executors in buying Bibles." There were also white slaves seated in the meeting-house. The "Connecticut Gazette" of January 5, 1764, advertised: "Just imported from Dublin in the brig Darby a parcel of Irish servants, both men and women, to be sold cheap by Israel Boardman at Stamford." These transports, as they were called, were sold into service for a period of years. An advertisement in the Boston "News-Letter" of the year 1727 says: "A Likely Servant Maid's Time of about Five Years, to be disposed of."

By men who sat in the colonial meeting-house the first Fugitive Slave Law was formed. This law became a part of the articles of confederation between all the New England colonies, and it ran thus: —

"If any servante rune away from his maister into another of these confederated jurisdictions, that in such case, upon ye certificate of one magistrate in ye jurisdiction out of which ye said servante fledd, or upon other due proofe, the said servante shall be delivered either to his maister or any other yt pursues brings such certificate or proofe."

As the Puritan legislators of New England professed to regulate their civil affairs in accordance with the laws of the Mosaic period of history, their Fugitive Slave Law should have been taken from the twenty-third chapter of Deuteronomy: "Thou shalt not deliver unto his master the servant which is escaped from his master unto thee."

The custom of "dignifying the meeting-house" was a source of envious feelings in social life. It created animosities between families, which descended from one generation to another, and which were kept alive by the formula of prayer repeated from the pulpit every Sunday for "our superiors, inferiors, and equals." It lingered after the colonial era had ended; and the last that was seen of it was in the secluded parish of Norfolk, Connecticut, in the year eighteen hundred and seventy-five.

VII.

THE WRETCHED BOYS.

"PUBLIC sermons do very little edify children," was one of the wise sayings of Martin Luther. The New England colonists did not think so, for they took their children to the meeting-house on Sunday, where they cast them out of the family circle and placed them under the surveillance of the town. This act appears to have been necessary because the boys, and sometimes the girls, were habitually a pest to the minister and a nuisance to the dignitaries of the parish. The popular disgust was expressed by a vote of Duxbury, in the year 1760, to choose a committee to take care of "the wretched boys on the Lords day." Certain laws enacted at the close of King Philip's war, to promote a better observance of the Sabbath in the Massachusetts colony, declared that the war had been caused by the behavior of those "wretched boys;" that, to quote its words, the war was a punishment of the colony for the "disorder and rudeness of youth in many congregations in time of the worship of God, whereby sin and profaneness is greatly increased." But, in defense of the boys, it is to be noticed that "sin and profaneness" were always increasing in the jaundiced eyes of the legislators of those days; and as a scapegoat for the increase was needed, there was none so easy to be taken as the boys. John Eliot, minister at Roxbury, expressed the opinion that boys had done nothing to provoke the war; that wars and disturbances in the meeting-house were a judgment on the people for wearing wigs.

Boys had been disturbers of the services of worship in the colonial meeting-house, and had been subject to police inspection. "tyme out of mynd." In the year 1666, John Dawes, who years before had been an officer "to oversee youth" in the North meeting-house of Boston, was empowered to take care of all persons "that ar disorderly in the time of God sollem worship, to compel such as ar without doors to goe into the metting hous & such as ar disorderly within with a small wand to correct them." In the next century the town of Harwich was ordering that the three hindmost benches in the meeting-house be reserved for boys under twelve years old, and three benches in the gallery for older boys ; and two men were appointed " to look after" these boys " that they sit in their seats and be kept from playing." In the year 1714, the deacons of Farmington were requested " to appoint persons who shall sit convenient to inspect the youth in the Meeting House on days of publick Worship and keep them in order."

The men appointed "to look after the boys" were called Inspectors of Youths ; in some towns they were called Wardens. They were not tithingmen, who were colony officers ;[1] they were simply policemen

[1] In the report of a Committee of the General Court, read March 26, 1697, the duties of tythingmen were recited in detail : " Yr Duty in presenting to the Justices the names of all such as Continue Tipling in Inns, & other publicque houses of entertainment especially on the Lords Day; and such as they find Drunke together with those that entertaine them ; all profane swears, and Cursers

of the meeting-house, and were paid by the town for their services. John Pike, of Dedham, was paid sixteen shillings, in the year 1723, for "keeping the boys in subjection six months." When he was hired a second time, he doubled his price. Thomas Wells was hired by the vestry of Christ Church in Boston to "sett in the Galleries and keep the boys in order." In a Cape Cod town, John King was appointed to keep boys "from playing and prophaning the Sabbath day;" and the town voted "to stand by the said John King" if he found it necessary to strike a boy in the exercise of his authority. This task was too much for the said John alone, and therefore the town appointed four men "to take care of the boys on Lords day and whip them if found playing." At Truro, three men were appointed "to whip boys that are disorderly on Sabbath days at or about

and the Number as nere as they Can of their oaths; All such as are guilty of extortion; All such as Keep houses where unlawful Games are used & such as sell Drinke without Lycence; the names of such as live Idley without estates, Suspicious persons, Whores, night Walkers, mothers of Bastard Children; Such as Commit Common Nuisances."

the meeting house." Not long after this action, it was ordered "that the town's powder be dried," as if a bloody contest with the rising generation was expected. These are illustrations of a state of things existing in every parish of New England.

As some men had the town's authority to flog other men's boys in the meeting-house, I may conclude that some parents allowed their children to run wild as ran their steers. Such a freedom was perhaps necessary in families of many children, numbering twelve, eighteen, or twenty-four. When all these were boys, the emaciated, careworn mother was doubtless glad to send off a lot of them to sea. As touching this subject, I copy the following news item from the New Haven "Chronicle" of March 13, 1787: —

"PORTSMOUTH N. HAMPSHIRE. There are now living in this town, a lady and gentleman who have not been married more than twenty years, and yet have eighteen sons; ten of whom are at sea, and eight at home with their parents."

Girls were wild also; for in Harwich it was voted "that the same course be pursued with the girls" as with the boys.

Did these men flog the girls? The over-burdened mothers could not send them to sea. Nor did the fathers trouble themselves much about the matter, except by resolutions in town meeting; for example, I read in the records of Farmington (1772): "Whereas Indecencies are practised by the young people in time of Publick Worship by frequently passing and repassing by one another in the Galleries; intermingling sexes to the great disturbance of many serious and well minded people — Resolved that each of us that are heads of Families will use our utmost endeavour to suppress the evils."

What did these colonial boys do to require so much police supervision? Through a rift in the records of Charlestown I can see some of their doings. They did not stand up, as the elders did, during the long prayers; they sat with their hats on "during ye whole exercise;" they sought opportunities to "run out of ye meeting house" while the preacher was preaching, or before "prayer be done and ye Blessing pronounced." I can guess the rest; they threw spitballs and nutshells to the bald heads below them; they shook props on the gallery benches; while the minister was praying, they were humming:

> "Noah built the ark,
> Shem he laid the floor,
> Japhet drave the geese in,
> And Ham he shut the door.
> Hey trixi rim! Hi trixi rim!
> I don't believe Old Noah could swim!
> Oh! nony, nony, no!"

A note-book of a Justice of the Peace in Connecticut, of the year 1750, specifies the behavior of a certain small meeting-house boy as follows: —

"A Rude and Idel Behaver in the meting hows Such as Smiling and Larfing and Intiseing others to the Same Evil

"Such as whispering and Larfing in the meting house between meetings

"Such as Larfing or Smiling and puling the heir of his nayber benoni Simkins in the time of publick Worship

"Such as playing with her Hand and fingers at her heir

"Such as throwing Sister penticost perkins on the Ice it being Saboth day or Lords day between the meting hous and his plaes of Abode."

The boys of colonial New England loom on us as the prototype of the "rough" of to-day, and I may imagine that within them was concealed a protoplasm of the American Revolution. Irreverence was born in their English blood. I have read in the churchwarden's accounts of the parish of St. Mary's, Reading, that, in the year 1600, Robert Marshall was paid twelve pence "to kepe the boyes & children out of the churche porche & churche yeard at service time," and that, in the year 1628, a seat was assigned "for John Gearey to loke to the boyes," and that, in the year 1652, the wardens agreed to "allow yearly to som one whome they shall think fitt Twentie shillings for looking to the boyes and keeping peace in the church," and "for tendinge the Churche door to still the Children."

In the colonial meeting-house Negroes and Indians made merriment for boys and girls. Look at Pomp Shorter in the Salem meeting-house when Benjamin Prescott was ordained, September 25, 1713. He is disorderly during divine service. He is brought down from his crib above the gallery, and is placed in a pew between two deacons who are seated under the eaves of the pulpit, where they are catching the drips of its theological shower. This trio in black and white is facing to the congregation. The venerable deacons welcome Pomp to their pew with that austere visage of Puritanism which is calculated to chill the mirth of human nature; but it does not close his laughing eyes which are turned up to the galleries, where boys and girls are peering at him over the edges. The situation is ludicrous; boys and girls begin to snicker; Pomp smiles a return; men and women looking on relax their meeting-house faces, and, for a moment, the air is infected with laughter. In that moment the men appointed to keep order are hustling around to find out who did it; and Pomp is set up in the broad alley to receive from the pulpit a severe condemnation for this "breach of the Sabbath" on a week day. When, in the year 1733, Philemon Robbins was ordained at Branford, Connecticut, whose population numbered 1600 including 130 negro slaves, the town ordered that "no negro servant shall be permitted to enter the meeting house." It wanted no Pomp Shorters present to make merriment for the boys.

VIII.

THE DISTURBERS OF PUBLIC WORSHIP.

THE principal disturbers of worship in the colonial meeting-house, besides boys, were dogs.

> "And in that town a dog was found,
> As many dogs there be,
> Both mongrel, puppy, whelp, and hound,
> And curs of low degree."

These dogs were regular attendants at the Sunday services. They went with the family; and as there was a good deal of sympathy between them and the wretched boys mentioned in the last chapter, they also were placed under discipline. At New London (1662), one of the duties of the sexton was "to order youth in the meeting-house and beat out dogs." At Charlestown (1666), a man was hired at four pounds a year "to ring the bell to meetings and to keep out dogs in meeting time." At Dedham (1674), a man was paid eight shillings a year "for keeping dogs out in meeting time and shutting the door." Andover did not object to dogs, but made them pay for the privilege of coming to meeting. The law of this town (1672) said: "Whatsoever dogs shall be in the meeting-house on the Sabbath day the owner thereof shall pay sixpence for every time." At Medford (1745), ten shillings was the price of a ticket to "any person who allows his dog to go into the meeting-house on the Sabbath day in the time of meeting." At Provincetown (1775), the law was to pay half a dollar or kill "every dog that comes into the meeting-house on the Sabbath day." At Abington (1793), those who took their dogs to meeting were ordered to pay "the same fine as for a breach of the Sabbath."

The dog law of Redding (1662) was peculiar. It ran thus: "Every dog that comes to the meeting either of Lord's day or lecture day, except it be their dogs that pays for a dog-whipper, the owner of those dogs shall pay sixpence for every time they come to the meeting that doth not pay the dog-whipper." Twenty-six men wrote their names, or made their marks, in the Redding records, agreeing to "pay the dog-whipper" to whip other people's dogs out of meeting, while their dogs remained and were recognized as members of the congregation in regular standing. Of course, boys and girls laughed, even at risk of punishment by His Majesty's justice of the peace, to see the dog-whipper pursuing heterodox dogs when they were running up and down aisles and gallery stairs, yelping as his whiplash fell upon them, but determined like their masters to stay in meeting until "ye exercise be ended."

The dog-whipper entered the colonial meeting-house from old England; where he was, like the constable, an important parochial officer, to whom in ancient times pieces of land were granted. In the parish records of Barton Turf in Norfolk, mention is made of the Dog-Whipper's Land. It is also stated that his duties consisted of "wiping ye dogges out of ye Churche." In the old church of Baslow is still preserved the whip of the dog-whipper of the parish. It is described as "a unique curiosity; it has a stout lash some three feet in length fastened to a short ash stick with leather bound round the handle."[1] In the register of Youlgreave Church, Derbyshire, of the year 1609, is a charge of sixteen pence paid to Robert Walton "for whipping ye dogges forth ye Church in time of Divyne Service." I have seen an action about church dogs older than that. The parish church of Reading, in the year 1570, agreed to pay John Marshall fourteen shillings a year; and "in consideration thereof he shalle from tyme to tyme se the churche cleane kepte, the seates swepte and cleane made, the mattes beten, the dogges driven owte."[2] That dogs were earnest churchgoers appears from the orders issued by Archbishop Laud, in the year 1636, which directed that the rail before the communion table shall be made "near one yard in height, so thick with pillars that dogs may not get in."

Dogs were a necessary part of the New England town community, because the neighboring woods harbored wolves and other wild beasts that preyed upon the

[1] Pendleton, *History of Derbyshire*.
[2] *Church Warden's Accounts of the Parish of St. Mary's, Reading, Berks;* 1550 to 1662.

flocks of sheep pasturing therein. Owners of large estates were required by town laws to keep "a sufficient. mastive dog," and owners of smaller estates to keep "a hound or beagle" for "the better fraying away wolves from the town." Bounties were paid for wild animals destroyed by dogs. The ears of a wildcat (the puma) would draw five shillings from the town treasury of Rehoboth, if properly certified. John Pierce got his certification in this way: he "brought a wildcat's head before the town and his ears were cut off by the constable before two selectmen." At Rochester the whole animal must be brought "to one of the selectmen with both thire ears" (the wildcat's ears) "on to be cut off." This course prevented cheating in wildcats. One sixpence was the Dedham town bounty for "an inch and a halfe of the end of a rattlesnake's tail with the rattle." A hundred years ago, foxes' heads were worth at Wareham, "three shillings for old ones, and one shilling for young ones puppied this year."

There were divers sorts of disturbances made in the colonial meeting-house. One at

Providence is described in the newspapers of June, 1725: "Some evil-minded persons placed a Sturgeon of about Eight feet in length on the Pulpit floor, where it lay undiscovered until the Lord's Day following; when it was so much Corrupted that it swarm'd with Vermine and caused such a Nausious and Infectious Stench that neither Minister nor People could by any Means Assemble in the Meeting House, which occasion'd them to perform their Exercise in the Orchard."

There was a disturbance of another sort in the meeting-house at Hopkinton, — "a Great Disturbance," it was called by Squire Harris, His Majesty's justice of the peace in and for the county of Middlesex, who made a note of it in his court record, saying that Richard Gibbon came before him and "complained of Jason Walker and set forth that on Lord's Day the 15th of January, 1743, Being in the Public Meeting house in Hopkinton in the forenoon there was a Great Disturbance which caused the Reverend Mr Barritt to Cease Preaching for some time. And that the complainant, one of the Deputy Sheriffs of the County, was commanded by John Jones Esquire to carry the Disturbers out of the meeting house; and that he Indeavored to obey the command, but Being Resisted by one Nathaniel Smith, he ordered Jason Walker in his majesty's name to assist him in carrying the said Nathaniel out of the meeting house, who absolutely Refused to give aid or assistance." Four other men — John Wood, Thomas Pierce, Eben Claflin, and Joseph House, Jr. — were convicted, at the same time, as promotors of this "Great Disturbance;" the cause of which no one now knoweth.

In the early years of the Massachusetts colony, the people called Quakers were disturbers of worship in the meeting-house. Although they had a keen sense of the superstition and tyranny of the Puritan government, they would have been a harmless and quiet people had they been left to themselves. Whittier says of the Quaker of the olden time : —

> "He walked by faith and not by sight,
>   By love and not by law;
> The pressure of the wrong or right
>   He rather felt than saw."

By order of the General Court, these people were imprisoned, branded with hot iron, whipped with pitched ropes, and banished from the colony. In the meeting-house at Boston, one was provoked to break a glass bottle and shout to the minister, "Thus will the Lord break you in pieces!" Another, whose name was Lydia Wardwell, walked, in the garb of Eden, into the Newbury meeting-house to show to the people the spiritual nakedness of their rulers. So severe was the feeling of the magistrates against Quakers that, in August, 1659, Thomas Macy, of Salisbury, who fled to Nantucket and there established a peaceful community, was called to account by the General Court for the simple act of showing the way to four travelers of that sect who stopped at his door on a rainy morning. He answered the court, saying: —

"On a rainy morning there came to my house Edward Wharton and three men more; the said Wharton spoke to me, saying they were travelling eastward, and desired me to direct them in the way to Hampton, and asked me how far it was to Casco Bay. I never saw any of the men before except Wharton, neither did I inquire their names or what they were ; but by their carriage I thought they might be Quakers and told them so, and desired them to pass on their way, saying to them I might possibly give offence in entertaining them ; and as soon as the rain ceased (for it rained very hard) they went away, and I never saw them since. The time they stayed in the house was about three quarters of an hour, but I can safely affirm it was not an hour. They spoke not many words in the time neither was I at leisure to talk with them, for I came home wet to the skin immediately before they came to the house, and I found my wife sick in bed. If this does not satisfy the Honored Court I am subject to their sentence."

In the following October, two of these weather-beaten travelers were hung on Boston Common, and were buried there. At the same time, Mary Dyer, an elderly woman, stood under a gallows, a rope around her neck. On the entreaty of her family she was given forty-eight hours in which to depart out of Massachusetts, with the threat that after the period, if found therein, she would be hung. In an order of the General Court all these victims were described as

"Quakers now in prison for theire rebellion, sedition, and presumptious obtruding themselves upon us."

At that time, the Common was a field of fifty or sixty acres, in which cows were pastured; they drank from a miry spring where the Frog Pond now is, and on warm days they ruminated in the shade of an elm-tree near by. The forest that once covered the Common had been cut away for firewood. Wild bushes and thickets, with many grassy hills, slopes, and vales, adorned its landscape. Its western edge was washed by the tides where Charles Street now runs, and eastward its acres extended to the site of the Tremont House. It was a "pleasant Common," said an old chronicler, where "Gallants a little before sunset walk with their marmalet madams till the nine o'clock bell rings, then home to their respective habitations; when presently the constables walk their rounds to see good orders kept and to take up locse people." On that October day when Quakers were to be hung, the gallants and their madams, the constables and the loose people, were probably there to see the barbarous exhibition and to hear the beating of the drums that drowned the words of dying men; for the hard heart of the General Court had ordered "Capt. James Oliver with one hundred souldiers taken proportionally out of each company in Boston, armed with pike and musketteers, with powder and bullet, to lead them to the place of execution and there see them hang until they be dead."

In June of the next year, Mary Dyer, having been found in Boston, was hung on the Common. There is still in existence a tear-stained letter written by her husband to Governor Endicott, pleading for "the life of my deare wife." It ends with these words:

"Oh let mercies wings once more soar above justice ballance and then whilst I live shall I exalt your goodness. But otherwise twill be a languishing sorrowe, yea soe great that I should gladly suffer the blow att once muche rather. I shall forbear to trouble your Honors with words, — neither am I in a capacitye to expatiate myselfe at present. I only say this, yourselves have been and are or may be husbands to wife or wives, and so am I — yea to one most dearlye beloved. Oh do not deprive me of her, but I pray give her me out again and I shall bee soe much obliged forever that I shall endeavour continually to utter my thanks. Pitye me. I beg it with tears."

Mary Dyer became one of the ghosts of Boston. Was it to her that Cotton Mather referred when, in November, 1716, he wrote in his diary: "There has lately appeared in Town an apparition of a Dead person. It is a thing so well attested that there can be no room to doubt it." There is a tradition that, after long intervals, Mary Dyer has appeared on the Common, dressed in gray garments of the fashion of a former time, her pale face showing the tender expressions of a noble life; and when spoken to she has vanished from sight. The story is, that in the twilight of an evening of October she appeared, and seated herself on a bench beside an old man, and said to him: "This is the fairest day of the year, and this Common is the fairest place in the world; for here in October of the year of our Lord 1659, Marmaduke Stevenson and William Robinson offered up their lives that the minds and consciences of men might be free in Massachusetts."

In March, another banished Quaker was

caught in Boston and was hung on the Common. Public opinion then declared itself against these barbarities, and the ruling mandarins of Massachusetts, having received words of disapproval from the King, were compelled to yield to it.

And there were men and women who made disturbances by noisy sleeping in the meeting-house. It was customary at Boston for a man, who carried a staff with a solid ball on the end of it, to walk about the house and knock up the sleepers. The process of getting asleep has been described in the journal of a man who slept for a living: first you become dull to sounds, then you become drowsy, then you are yawning, then you are nodding, then you are turning for a position, then you are asleep; and soon a snore summons the watchman, who arouses you by a tap on your head with the ball; or, if you are a woman whose head is concealed under a bonnet, he wakes you by brushing your face with a fox's tail.

A Sunday sleeper whose name has been preserved, and whose brave experience has amused many generations of his imitators, was Robert Scott of the Lynn congregation.

One Sunday he was hammered out of his nap so forcibly by a thud of the awakening ball that he jumped up and knocked down his assailant. For this offense he was taken to court and condemned to be severely whipped for "common sleeping" at the public exercise and for striking him that waked him. This "common sleeping" was not done in Puritan meeting-houses only. The people called Friends, whose preachers preached not of Mount Sinai but of the deceitfulness of the human heart, gave themselves up to the same enjoyment. The records of the South Kingstown Meeting in Rhode Island mention the appointment of overseers who were charged to suppress "Sleeping and other indecencies" in their meeting-house.[1]

Congregations in Old England were also sleepy, and they required a "sluggard, waker," as the churchwardens of Castleton in Derbyshire designated the man to whom they paid ten shillings, in the year 1722, for arousing sleepers "by tapping them over the head with a wand." But Sir Roger de Coverley, who, as Addison tells us, was

[1] *Thomas Hazard son of Robt, call'd College Tom: a Study of Life in Narragansett in the XVIIIth Century.*

landlord to the whole congregation, allowed no sluggard-waker to be employed; "for if by chance he has been surprised into a short nap at sermon, upon recovering out of it he stands up and looks about him, and if he sees anybody else nodding, either wakes them himself, or sends his servant to them."

It has been said that sleepiness in the meeting-house can be accounted for on scientific principles; that it is a condition of hypnotism, indicating a complete absorption of the sermon instead of inattention to it. Fixing your mind on the voice of the preacher produces the conditions necessary to domination by his mind; the drooping eyelids and nodding heads do not indicate the preacher's dullness, but are testimonials of his powerful influence over those who are fast asleep. Whatever may be the philosophy of it, the fact remains that on Sunday the human nature of colonial New England seemed to close its eyes for a general drowse in the meeting-house. The sermon shuts off the incessant labors of the week past and of the week to come, as a barrier reef shuts off from a sleepy lagoon —

"The long wash of Australasian seas."

IX.

THE NEIGHBORS OF THE MEETING-HOUSE.

GIDEON Buckingham advertised in the "Connecticut Journal," February 7, 1791 : "To be Sold. A Dwelling House Pleasantly situated in Milford within a few Rods of the Meeting House, in which has been kept a Tavern for a great Number of Years."

As the colonial meeting-house stood in the centre of the town, a tavern was always its neighbor. This was a place of general resort; to it town meetings were sometimes adjourned; in it politicians, idlers, and train-band captains made their headquarters. Here selectmen held court attended by the town clerk, who wrote in the town book such sales and transfers as were brought in, together with marriages, deaths, estrays, and earmarks. The town clerk was not a pink of learning. As an illustration of his struggles with words of more than one syllable, I copy his record from the Rochester book: "Joseph Benson's disstiniguishin marke is a hole in ye nigh eare and a slit in ye top of ye Right eare in Aug ye 1 : 1699."

Men, like sheep, are gregarious. They went to taverns to spend their evenings because the village offered no other form of social amusement. This habit of tavern haunting, as it was called by those who condemned it, became so general that a convention of ministers at Boston, in May, 1694, declared it to be a sin; they said: "Ye Liberty taken by Towne Dwellers to mispend their Time in Tavernes which are places properly & honestly designed but for ye Accommodation of Travellers — It is most earnestly pray'd That some effectuall check may be given unto this way of sinning." And yet the village parson was often to be seen there of an evening.

The tavern door stands open; let us peep in, after sundown, when the gossips have come and taken their accustomed places in the bar-room. Among them you may see such types of the English family as have been portrayed by Shakespeare, Fielding, and Bunyan. Here is Falstaff drinking sack-posset, telling stories, and falling into great laughter. Parson Adams comes in and discourses with Talkative the son of Saywell, who "will talk when on the alebench of religious matters, and the more drink he hath in his crown the more of these things he hath in his mouth." Mr. Facingbothways is here, supporting both sides of an argument; and Mr. Fairspeech is here, and Mr. Anything agreeing with everybody while he fumbles in his pockets for a coin with which to pay his score. These men are samples of the men of the village. They all do the same things, think the same thoughts, speak the same drawl, tell the same stories, and spend much time in the tavern, year in and year out. And so each evening passes, until the low-ceiled room is filled with the incense of tobacco, the candles are burning to a splutter, and the meeting-house bell strikes nine o'clock. Then the landlord pulls down and locks the pickets which inclose the bar, and the loungers walk silently away to their homes. It was in the bond which he gave on receiving from the Court of Common Pleas a license to keep the tavern, that he would not "suffer any children or servant or other person to remain in his house tippling or drinking after nine o'clock in the night."

The landlord's business belongs to the family. His father kept the tavern; and should his wife outlive him she will keep it, until, in turn, the son succeeds to the inheritance. You may read in the churchyard the sculptured story: —

> "Beneath this stone, in hopes of Zion,
> There lies the landlord of the Lion.
> His wife keeps on the business still,
> Resigned unto the Heavenly will."

The pound harboring stray cattle was a neighbor of the meeting-house. It was thirty feet square and six or seven feet high; the first public structure built in the town. Other neighbors were the whipping-post, the stocks, the pillory, and the wooden horse; instruments of punishment which were adapted to the various incidents of colonial life. David Linnell and Hannah Shelly, of Barnstable, who confessed fornication, were flogged at the post "by sentence of the magistracy." Sometimes there was a merciful thought in such punishments; as when Sarah Osgood, of Newbury, was sentenced "to be whipped twenty stripes for fornication within six weeks after she shall be brought to bed." Thieves were flogged and then sent to jail. No culprit was beaten with more than forty stripes, and it was forbidden by law that "any true gentleman be punished with whipping unless his crime be very shameful and his course of life viscious and profligate." It is worthy of note that the position of the whipping-post and stocks was similar to that which they occupied in the time of the prophet Jeremiah: "Then Pashur smote Jeremiah the prophet, and put him in the stocks that were by the house of the Lord."

Men of the trainband who were absent from the ranks on a training-day, and had not paid the fines in which they were condemned by a justice of the peace, were favored with a seat on the wooden horse in presence of a general muster. There was a fitness in using the wooden horse to punish a horse thief; I find such a use reported in a New Haven newspaper of January 16, 1787: —

"Last Tuesday one James Brown, a transient Person was brought to the Bar of the County Court on a complaint for Horsestealing — being put to plead — plead guilty, and on Thursday received the sentence of the Court, that he should be confined to the Goal in this County 8 Weeks, be whipped the first Day 15 stripes on the naked Body, and set one Hour on the wooden Horse, and on the first Monday of each following Month be whipped ten stripes, and set one hour at each time on the wooden Horse."

They swore terribly in colonial times. A law of Massachusetts of the year 1692 said that every person who shall "profanely sware or curse" is to pay a fine of five shillings or sit in the stocks two hours. The fine was also to be "twelve pence for every oath after the first." John Hull instructed his captains when they sailed from Boston that they must pray and not swear at sea, lest the Lord send foul blasts to wreck his ships. A law of the year 1746, "to more effectually prevent profane cursing and swearing," was ordered to be read in the meeting-house by ministers "on the Lord's day next succeeding the choice of town officers yearly."

A prisoner in the stocks could take to himself the consolation of Tertullian, were he familiar with the writings of that ecclesiastic, who said, "The leg feels nothing in the stocks when the mind is in heaven." But the colonial swearers and slanderers were not set therein because of heavenly qualifications. The legs of Jane Boulton, of Plymouth, were locked in the stocks because she had uttered too many reviling speeches. Idlers standing outside the meeting-house at Eastham were set in the stocks because they would not attend the services of worship. The selectmen of Portsmouth, to protect prisoners in the stocks from being pelted with products of kitchen gardens, built their stocks within a cage, and set the pillory on top of it, and then they placed the machine at the west end of the meeting-house. The rulers of those times had no thought of the sacredness of the human body, which St. Paul declared to be "the temple of the Holy Ghost," when they nailed a man to the pillory by his ears and publicly flogged his naked body. Punishment by the pillory was considered to be infamous. In the year 1697, William Vesey, of Braintree, was sentenced to the pillory for ploughing on a thanksgiving day, and for declaring that James the Second was King, instead of

William, for whose escape from assassination the thanksgiving was appointed. Five years later he was elected a member of the General Court; but he was expelled because he had suffered infamous punishment in the pillory.

The heyday of all these barbarous instruments was Thursday, known throughout New England as lecture day, when attendance to hear "the fifth day lecture" was as compulsory as was attendance to hear the sermons on Sunday. This service was introduced to the colonies by John Cotton, who brought it with him from Boston in Old England, where he had maintained his "ordinary lecture every Thursday" in St. Butolph's under direction of the Bishop of Lincoln. The day was first mentioned in New England history by Governor Winthrop, in connection with the opening of a market in Boston. He wrote, on the 4th of March, 1634: "By order of Court a mercate was erected at Boston to be kept upon Thursday the fifth day of the week, being lecture day." The reverence in which this day was held may be seen in the records of John Cotton's church, wherein a rehearsal of the misdemeanors of a poor excommunicated soul included his "sometimes forsaking the Lecture." In the year 1679, there was made in Boston "an order and advice of ye magistrates yt all the elders of this towne might jointly carry on the 5th day Lecture." It then became popular in all the towns of New England. It was held near the noon hour; schools, if there were any, were dismissed and labor was suspended, so that no one should be deprived of the privilege of attending the lecture.

Samuel Sewall speaks of a lecture day in midwinter of the year 1715 when a northeast snowstorm was raging in Boston and, in spite of the storm, there were two hundred men and sixteen women present at the lecture. He counted them because the attendance was small. At these meetings the names of those persons of the town who were intending to be married were called aloud. This gave a little zest to the occasion. Doubtless a greater zest was given by the fact that somebody was to be set up in the pillory, or locked in the stocks, or flogged at the whipping-post, or publicly corrected before the congregation.

The Connecticut Records tell of a lecture-day sentence passed upon Nicholas Olmsteed: "He is to stand uppon the Pillory at Hartford the next lecture day dureing the time of the lecture. He is to be sett on a lytle before the begining & to stay thereon a litle after the end." But Walter Gay, who had been courting the parson's maid, is allowed to hear the lecture, and then, for his labor of love, he is to stand up in the meeting-house and be scolded from the pulpit, — "publiquely corrected for his misdemeanor in laboring to inveagle the affections of Mr Hoockers mayde." An impudent servant is brought from prison every week, on lecture day, after the lecture is ended, to receive scoldings, until the scolder gets tired of the occupation. The story is this: "Susan Coles for her rebellious cariedge toward her mistris is to be sent to the howse of correction and be keept at to hard labour & course dyet to be brought forth the next lecture day to be publiquely corrected and so to be corrected weekley until Order be given to the contrary." With these little weekly comedies Thursday Lecture was made a popular institution in colonial New England.

The stocks, the whipping-post, and the pillory — all intended (quoting the historic English) "to punyssche trasgressours Ageynste ye Kyngs Maiesties lawes" — came from Old England. They stood near every parish church. John Taylor, a rhymester known as the water poet, tells us that about the year 1630 —

"In London, and within a mile, I ween,
 There are jails and prisons full eighteen,
 And sixty whipping-posts and stocks and cages."

It is on record that, in the year 1287, the Lord Mayor of London "did sharpe correction make upon bakers for making bread of light weight;" as bakers make bread now without any sharp correction. He caused divers of them to be put in the pillory, as also one Agnes Dantie "for selling of mingled butter." Agnes was, apparently, the first dealer in oleomargarine. A pillory in Cornhill was not unlike that which the selectmen of Portsmouth set up at the west end of the meeting-house, and claimed as their own invention. It is described as a timbered cage with stocks attached to it and a pillory on top of it; three instruments of torture in one. The use of this machine was offered to "bakers offending in the assize of bread;" to "millers stealing of corn at the mill;" to "balds, scolds, and other offenders." It is well known what the scold was; her companion the bald was a poor fellow who had neither dignity, nor money, nor a soul above meanness. Some scolds and balds came to New England. The "other offenders" for whom a pillory stood waiting were sometimes of a high grade. For example: Dr. Bostwick, for a publication ending with the prayer —

"From plague, and pestilence, and famine,
From bishops, priests, and deacons,
Good Lord, deliver us!"

was deposed from the ministry, was branded and whipped, then his nostrils were slit and his ears cropped in the pillory at Westminster. But his loving wife was there. A letter written at the time says: "He stood two hours in the pillory, his wife got on a stool and kissed him. His ears being cut off she called for them, put them in a clean handkerchief and carried them away with her." The grim founders of New England did as much for Baptists and Quakers, and others who spoke their minds about the magistrates.

"It is ordered," by the General Court at Boston, June 14, 1631, "that Philip Ratliffe shall be whipped, have his eares cut off, fined 40 pounds, and banished out of the limits of this jurisdiction, for uttering malicious and scandalous speeches against the Government." There was but one political party in those days.

X.

THE COMEDY AND TRAGEDY OF THE PULPIT.

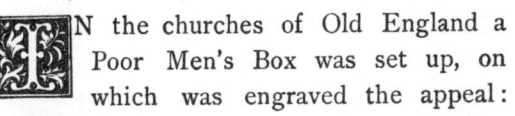

IN the churches of Old England a Poor Men's Box was set up, on which was engraved the appeal: "Remember the poor, and God will bless thee and thy store." It is written in the churchwarden's accounts of St. Mary's, Reading, of the year 1627: "Payde to Iohn Gripp the Joiner for making the poore mans box and the bannesters to it 8 shillings." This box was not seen in the colonial meeting-house. People who sat on its hard benches heard but little of that sympathetic preaching which impels men and women

"To scorn the sordid world."

There was a Society, on whose behalf sermons were preached, "For Propagating Christian Knowledge to carry the Gospel to the

Aboriginal Natives on the Borders of New England;" but there were no temperance societies; no missionary societies sending teachers of the gospel into foreign lands.

Colonial preachers had an aptitude for riding hobby-horses. Mr. Davenport, at New Haven, preached that men must take off their hats and stand up at the announcement of the text. Mr. Williams, at Salem, preached that women must wear veils during the exercises of public worship. Mr. Cotton, at Boston, preached that women ought to be ashamed to wear veils in the meeting-house; that married women had no pretense to wear them as virgins, and that neither married nor unmarried women would choose to wear them by the example of Tamar the harlot; nor need they wear veils for such purpose as did Ruth in her widowhood.

In the year 1684, Increase Mather preached at Boston that "Gynecandrical Dancing or that which is commonly called Mixt or Promiscuous Dancing of Men and Women, be they elder or younger persons together, cannot be tolerated in such a place as New England without great Sin." His argument was:

"Promiscuous Dancing is a breach of the

seventh Commandment, as being an occasion and an incentive to that which is evil in the sight of God. There are Scriptures which seem expressly and particularly to condemn the Dancing we plead against. It is spoken of as the great sin of the Daughters of Sion, that they did walk with stretched out necks, and with wanton eyes, walking and mincing as they go, and making a tinkling with their feet.— Isaiah 3. 16."

"Who were the Inventors of Petulant Dancings? Learned men have well observed that the Devil was the first inventor of the impleaded Dances, and the Gentiles who worshipped him the first Practitioners of this Art. They sat down to eat and drink, and rose up to play, or to dance."

And so the preacher went on, drawing upon imagination for his facts, until he came to the plea that "Miriam danced and David danced," according to the Scriptures. To which his answer was, "Those Instances are not at all to the purpose!" There must have been many hearers in the meeting-house whose common sense caused them to smile at such reasoning. Mixed dancing had become popular in Boston. Samuel Sewall, writing November 12, 1685, says:

"The ministers of this Town Come to the Court and complain against a Dancing Master who seeks to set up here and hath mixt Dances; and his time of Meeting is Lecture Day. And 't is reported he should say that by one Play he could teach more Divinity than Mr. Willard or the Old Testament." Mr. Willard was the minister of the Old South Church. The Puritan prejudice against dancing was ineradicable. At New Haven, in the year 1784, when a dancing master had advertised to teach his art and had secured patrons, an attempt was made to expel him from the town.

Mr. Mather preached also against wearing periwigs. A young woman of Rhode Island, named Hetty Shepard, when visiting at Boston, in the year 1676, wrote in her diary: "I could not help laughing at the periwig of Elder Jones which had gone awry. The periwig has been greatly censured as encouraging worldly fashions not suitable to the wearing of a minister of the gospel, and it has been preached about by Mr. Mather and many think he is not severe enough in the matter, but rather doth find excuse for it on account of health."

In the year 1722, Solomon Stoddard, minister at Northampton, said: "Hooped Petticoats have something of Nakedness; Mixt Dances are incentives to lust." In a sermon to men on the sin of wearing long hair, Mr. Stoddard reasoned as follows:—

"It is utterly Unlawful to wear their Hair long. It is a great Burden and Cumber; it is Effiminancy, and a vast Expence. One Scripture that condemns it, 1 Cor. 11. 14. Doth not even nature itself teach you that if a man wear long hair it is a shame to him? That which the light of Nature condemns is a Moral Evil. . . . Moreover, in the next verse the apostle shows that Nature teaches Women to wear their Hair long. He saith, If a woman have long hair it is a glory to her, for her hair is given her for a covering, but not to Men. Another Scripture doth also condemn it, viz. Ezek. 44. 20. Neither shall they shave their heads, nor suffer their locks to grow long, they shall only poll their heads. Here are two extreams forbid; shaving the head, and suffering their locks to grow long. This must either signify some spiritual thing, but no man knows what; or some Gospel Institution; and if so, why is it not enjoyned unto ministers in the New Testament? Or else it is a Moral Law; and so it must be. One part of it is surely moral; They shall not shave their heads; therefore the other part is Moral also; They shall not suffer their locks to grow long."

The style of women's apparel was a favorite topic with colonial preachers. Addison says that women in "their thoughts are ever turned upon appearing amiable to the other sex; they talk, and move, and smile, with a design upon man; every feature of their faces, every part of their dress, is filled with snares and allurements." In the light of this truth it is difficult to understand what was the matter at Abington, in the year 1775, when the men of the town "Voted that it is an indecent way that the female sex do sit with their hats and bonnets on to worship God in his house." Perhaps they were feathered women whose headdresses were adorned with dead and stuffed birds; or perhaps their hats and bonnets were so lofty and large that men who sat behind them were shut off from a view of the pulpit and the preacher. Whichever it may have been, the women of to-day who read this line of history will feel an inward cry of nature asserting their kinship with those women of Abington town.

Fashions in other things, besides veils, hair, petticoats, hoops, hats, and bonnets, attracted theological attention. The pretty woman in Hogarth's picture of "The Sleeping Congregation" represents the truth of the adage that the sense of being well-dressed gives to woman a feeling of satisfaction which religion is powerless to bestow. Her flowing robes and the low cut of her corsage reveal "snares and allurements" which were the captivating fashion of her time, both in Old England and in New England. She is seated near enough to the foot of the lofty pulpit to catch every word that falls from the lips of the droning preacher; but her hands are listless in her lap, her uncovered head is slightly tilted back, her eyes are closed, she is softly sleeping. Near by sits the sensuous and bewigged parish clerk; one of whose eyes is winking under the pressure of sleep, and the other is struggling to keep its sight upon the slumbering beauty.

They were women, even if they were Calvinists. They laughed at the fashions in dress of other days, as women laugh now, and adopted them whenever they came around again. They wore large hoops, peaked stomachers, and modesty pieces, if in style; and "laid their breasts bare in the meeting-house." Then came the sermons. Let us turn to one that was preached by George Weekes at Harwichtown during the fashions in dress of the Hogarth period. Of course this minister knew nothing of the theories of modern art: that there is a vast difference between the naked and the nude; that, although an uncultivated mind can appreciate the immodesty of nakedness, only an educated mind can understand the purity of the nude. He preached his own theory, and I will give his argument:—

"*First.* The Sin of our first Parents hath occasioned a necessity for our wearing of Cloths whilst we live in this world."

"*Secondly.* As Clothing is now necessary, so there is a necessity that our Cloths should be made in some fashion. To make a Garment without any shape or fashion is not possible."

"*Thirdly.* It is not necessary that people in all Ages nor that all persons in an Age; nor that one and the same person should at all times keep invariably to one and the same fashion. . . . There is no law which obliges people in every Generation to keep to one and the same fashion:—where there is no law there is no transgression. (Romans, 5 : 11.)"

"*Fourthly.* We should take heed, that we become not guilty of breaking the sixth Command by following such fashions as have a tendency to destroy our Health. We should take heed, least we provoke God to anger against us by following such fashions as are contrary to the seventh Commandment."

"And therefore it is, that I have been and am still of the mind, that Women by wearing their Hoops, and laying their Breasts bare, become guilty of breaking the seventh Commandment."

The preacher, continuing the sermon, turns his attention from the women to the men of the congregation. He attacks their wigs by propounding this question: "If a Man cut off his hair to wear a Perriwig, merely because it is a common fashion, or because he dislikes the color of his own hair; or if he cover his head with such a Perriwig as doth disfigure him, doth he not therein walk contrary to God's law? (Deuteronomy, 6: 5. Matthew, 22: 37.)"

"*Firstly.* Adam, so long as he continued in innocency, did wear his own Hair, and not a Perriwig. Indeed, I do not see how it was possible that Adam should dislike his own hair, and therefore cut it off, so that he might wear a Perriwig, and yet have continued innocent."

"*Secondly.* When the Son of God appeared in flesh, he did not from a dislike of his own Hair, cut it off to wear a Perriwig. The Lord Jesus always did those things that pleased his Father; but if he had found fault with his own Hair, and had therefore cut it off to wear a Perriwig, he would have dishonored his Father; therefore, 't is evident that he did wear his own Hair and not a Perriwig."

"*Thirdly.* The Children of God will not wear Perriwigs after the Resurrection. The Body of Christ did not consume, nor his Hair wast in the Grave: he doubtless now wears the Hair that is essential to his own head. And the bodies of Believers shall then doubtless be adorn'd with Hair essential to their own heads."

"*Fourthly.* We have no warrant in the word of God, that I know of, for our wearing of Perriwigs except it be in extraordinary cases. . . . Elisha did not cover his head with a Perriwig, altho' it was bald."

"To see the greater part of Men in some congregations wearing Perriwigs is a matter of deep lamentation. For either all these men had a necessity to cut off their Hair, or else not. If they had a necessity to cut off their Hair, then we have reason to take up a lamentation over the sin of our first Parents which hath occasion so many Persons in one Congregation, to be sickly, weakly, crazy Persons. Oh, Adam, what has thou done!"

The name of the author of this sermon is preserved in "Weeke's Hollow;" the place in Harwich where he perished during a winter's night of the year 1744.

That was the comedy side of the pulpit; there was also a tragedy side. Some preachers announced to their congregations that infants were lost; that certain dead persons were in hell; that, despite the experience of St. Paul, God could easier convert the seat on which they were sitting than convert a moral man; that the unconverted have no right to sing Psalms; that there are sinners for whom Christ did not die. Some evolved doctrinal teachings from very trivial subjects. If a man fell into a well, or was thrown from a horse, or was drowned in a river, the event brought forth a homily. Solomon Williams, of Lebanon, Connecticut, preached a sermon in September, 1741, "On the sudden Death of John Woodward who was drowned in passing the Ferry at Haddam, and on the Deliverance of Sam Gray." A man about to be hung was ceremoniously brought into the meeting-house to hear the last sermon of his lifetime, in which he was probably told, "'T is a thousand to one if ever thou be one of that small number whom God hath picked out to escape the wrath to come!" Such sermons were printed with a thrilling narrative of the bloody deeds of the criminals, and they were the only exciting reading which people could get. Benjamin Coleman, minister at Boston, preached a sermon in July, 1726, "to the late Miserable Pirates on the Lord's Day before their Execution," which was printed with its piratical story before the week was ended. Then the body of the pirate captain was hanging in chains from a gibbet set on the ledge of Nix's Mate, at the entrance of Boston harbor; whither the story readers could go and look at it; and where for years it swung in the easterly gales, a reminder of the fate of evil-doers on the sea.

Thomas Hooker, one of the most noted of the early colonial ministers, was called "a Son of Thunder," and was eulogized by his contemporaries as

"A pourer forth of lively Oracles;
In saving souls, the sum of Miracles."

In one of his stirring sermons he said to his congregation: "Suppose any soule here present were to behold the damned in hell, and if the Lord should give thee a little peepe-hole into hell that thou did'st see the horror of those damned soules, and thy heart begins to shake in consideration thereof; then propound this to thy owne heart, what paines the damned in hell doe endure for sinne; and thy heart will shake and quake at it, the least sinne that ever thou didst commit, though thou makest a light matter of it, is a greater evill then the paines of the damned in hell. Men shrink at this and loathe to goe down to hell and to be in endlesse torments. Oh get you into the arke, the Lord Jesus; and when one is roaring and yelling — Oh the Devill, the Devill — another is ready to hang himselfe or to cut his own throat."

It was true; they were ready to hang themselves. Those "peepe-holes into hell" were opened to right of them and to left of them. The terrible doctrines continually trumpeted from the pulpit made hearers anxious about their future state. This anxiety, with the cheerless solitude of rural life, caused them to become morbid on religious subjects, and relief was sought by some in suicide. "She hung herself in the closet under the stairs;" or, "He went out to the barn and hung himself in the hayloft;" were stories told in many towns.

This condition of the public mind attracted attention in the legislature at Boston; where a law was enacted, October 16, 1660, whose preamble contained these words: "Considering how far Satan doth prevail upon persons within this Jurisdiction to make away with themselves." It was Satan, they said, not the sermonizings of the times, that induced the suicides. "To bear testimony against such wicked and unnatural practices," said the legislators, "that others may be deterred therefrom; Do order that if any person be wilfully guilty of their own Death, every such person shall be denied the privilege of being Buried in the Common Burying place of Christians, but shall be Buried in some Common Highway and a Cart-load of Stones laid upon the grave as a Brand of Infamy, and as a warning to others to beware of the like Damnable practices."

This history destroys the modern theory that "suicide is an evidence of culture;" although the vainglorious Cotton Mather contemplated suicide, if we may believe his own confession written on the 16th of March, 1703: "Should I tell in how many Forms the Devil has assaulted me it would strike my Friends with Horror. Sometimes Temptations to Impurities, and sometimes to Blasphemy and Atheism, and the Abandonment of all Religion as a mere Delusion, and sometimes to Self Destruction itself."

The law which I have quoted remained in force during one hundred and sixty-four years, or until February 21, 1824, when the

Governor of Massachusetts signed its repeal. And yet, on the isolated farms of New England, suicide continued to be the outcome of lives whose mental power had collapsed and whose hope had become extinct. Suicide was the last stage in the deterioration of a family stock which, for generations, had been nurtured on the doctrines of John Calvin.

XI.

THE POOR PARSONS.

THERE was a church as soon as the parson came. It was the association of a few devout men and women united by a covenant, without a doctrine or a creed. "We covenant with the Lord and one with another and we do bind ourselves in the presence of God to walk together in all his ways according as he is pleased to reveal himself unto us in his blessed word of truth;" so opened the first church covenant made in New England; beautiful in its simplicity.

In April, 1629, the Company of Massachusetts Bay, at London, having despatched ships to New England, wrote to its planters saying:—

"And for that the prpagating of the Gospele is the thing wee doe prfess aboue all to bee or ayme in settling this Plantacon, wee haue bin carefull to make plentyfull prvision of Godly Ministers, by whose faithfull preachinge godly conversacon, and exemplary lyfe, wee trust, not only those of or owne Nation wilbe built vp in the Knowledge of God, but also the Indians may in God's appointed tyme bee reduced to the obedyence of the Gospele of Christ."

The ships carried about three hundred colonists, with cows, goats, and horses, and also four ministers. One of the ministers was Francis Higginson, who had been educated at Cambridge University, and was preaching at Leicester as a minister of the Established Church when he received an invitation to embark "unto a voyage into New England," with kind promises to support him.[1] He set sail from London with feelings of sadness, for he loved "our deare native soyle of England;" and when they came to

[1] London, "23d March, 1628. At this meeting Intimation was given by Mr Nowell by letters ffrom Mr Izake Iohnson, that one Mr Higgeson of Lester, an Able minister prffers to goe to or plantacon; who being approved for a reverend grave minister, fitt for or present occasions, it was thought by thes present to entreat Mr Jno Humfrey to ride presently to Lester, and If Mr Higgeson may Conveniently be had to goe this present vioage that he should deale with him." — *Records of the Company of Massachusetts Bay.*

Land's End, he called his children to the stern of the ship and, with thoughts that did him honor, said: "Farewell, dear England! We do not go to New England as separatists from the Church of England, though we cannot but separate from the corruptions in it, but we go to practice the positive part of church reformation and propagate the Gospel in America." The Company, under an agreement with him to go to the colony, had paid to him forty pounds in money, and covenanted to pay to him yearly thirty pounds and give to him a house, firewood, the milk of two cows, and many acres of land. This was the beginning of that form of salary which, during two centuries, was the life-long reward of the poor parsons of New England. The Company also promised to him "a manservant to take care and look to his things and to catch him fish and foule and provide other things needful, and also two maidservants to look to his family."

He kept a journal of his voyage across the Atlantic, which presents a pleasing picture of the man who was so much of a philosopher that he wrote: "Those that love their owne chimney corner and dare not go farre beyond their own townes end shall never have the honour to see the wonderfull workes of Almighty God." During the first week at sea one of his children died; then the company kept "a solemn day of fasting and prayer unto God," and the sailors said they never heard of the like performed at sea before. He notes that the shipmaster "used every night to sett the 8 and 12 a clocke watches with singing a psalme and prayer that was not read out of a booke." He notes fair winds, and "boisterous winds blowing crosse," and "foggie and calmish" days, and "grampus fishes as bigg as an oxe," and great turtles and whales, and "scools of mackrill," and "a mountayne of ice shining as white as snow," — until, on the 27th of June, the ship entered what is now Gloucester harbor on Cape Ann. There, the journalist says, "was an island whither four of our men with a boate went and brought back again ripe strawberries and gooseberries, and sweet single roses."

By written ballots of the little church of the simple covenant (every man, as says a contemporary letter, "wrote in a note his name"), Francis Higginson became the first regular parson chosen in New England. After a service of less than a year he died of a hectic fever; leaving a repute like that of Chaucer's Poore Parson: —

> "Christes love and his apostles twelve
> He taught, but first he followed it himselve."

The popular judgment of New England about an educated parson was like that expressed in John Selden's "Table Talk:" "Without school divinity a divine knows nothing logically, nor will he be able to satisfy a rational man out of the pulpit." Colonial ministers were college-bred. Many of them were settled for life in small isolated parishes, where they found no books, no learning, no intellectual sympathies, no points of contact with the world at large; where they received "much, sometimes all of their scanty salary in kind, eking it out by the drudgery of a cross-grained farm."

In such parishes the parson's salary was rarely paid when it was due, and the amount of it was sometimes unmercifully cut down by the whimsical votes of town meetings, because parishioners who hoarded their small savings were apt to think that the parson was drawing too much money out of the town treasury, or too much substance out of the farms. He was permitted to use the glebe or "ministry lands" under conditions. A town in Barnstable County stipulated that if the parson "will fence with cedar" the ministry meadow, his heirs "may have the fence after his decease." That bargain was made in the year of our Lord 1715. The same shrewdness existed at Wareham in the year 1806, when the town voted "To procure Rales anuf to Fence the min ner stree Fresh meddo the Rev Noble Evrit to make the Fence & keep it in Repare." Nobody objected if he turned an honest penny by serving as the town's sweeper and fuller. It is less than a hundred years ago when the parson of Wareham was ekeing out his means of living by sweeping the meeting-house for a compensation of three dollars a year; and, as was customary, he did "winge or rub down the principal seats" on the day after sweeping; then he eked it out a little further by running a fulling mill in which, with pestles and stampers that rose and fell in troughs containing fuller's earth, he extracted grease from cloths homespun by women of his congregation. The parson might be the physician of his parish. For forty-five years did Samuel Palmer, of Falmouth, preach to the souls and practice on the bodies of his people. His gravestone says: "His Virtues would a Monument supply." At Gosport, on the Isles of Shoals, John Tuck was physician and parson for fifty years; so was John Avery, at Truro, for forty-four years. In Herbert's old book, "The Country Parson," we are told that a parson may become qualified to treat the ills that flesh is heir to by "Seeing one anatomy, reading one book of physic, and having one herbal by him." This was the extent of an education in physic which the poor parsons of New England possessed. Their tool was a lancet; their healing doses were herbs of the field and garden, carefully gathered and hung in the peak of the garret to be dried, which were believed to be more potent than the strong drugs of an apothecary. When they did not heal, it was the will of the Lord that they should not. Perhaps the parson's doses, when given "without money and without price," opened the way for a willing reception of his spiritual prescriptions.

The most noted of double-life parsons was Michael Wigglesworth who, for forty-nine years, was the physician of Maulden. He was noted because he was the author of that famous and dreadful Calvinian poem,—

The
DAY OF DOOM,
or
A Poetical Description of the
GREAT AND LAST JUDGMENT,
With a Short discourse About
ETERNITY.

In the poet's description of the Day of Judgment he says:—

"Then to the bar all they drew near
 Who died in infancy;
And never had, or good or bad,
 Effected personally."

These infants at the bar pleaded that they ought not to suffer for the guilt of Old Adam; for, said they,—

"Not we, but he, ate of the tree
 Whose fruit was interdicted."

To this the judge replied that none can suffer for what they never did;

"But, what you call old Adam's fall,
 And only his trespass,
You call amiss to call it his;
 Both his and yours it was.
He was designed of all mankind
 To be a public head,
A common root whence all should shoot,
 And stood in all their stead."

So the infants had no standing in court; and mothers, the reverend poet tells us, are not allowed in Heaven to distress themselves with thoughts about the babes who are suffering in that place where

"God's vengeance feeds the flame
With piles of wood, and brimstone flood,
 That none can quench the same."

Such was the sanguinary theology taught in the colonial meeting-house; whither the babe was carried by a midwife, on the first Sunday after birth, to be rescued by baptism from a terrible destiny.

Near the stone wall which bounds the Bell Rock cemetery in the ancient town where Michael Wigglesworth preached and practiced physic stands his gravestone. Strange to say, his famous poem, which Cotton Mather said would become immortal, is not mentioned in the inscription: —

Memento Mori : Fugit Hora.
Here Lyes Buried ye Body of
That Faithful Servant of
Jesus Christ ye Reverend
Mr. MICHAEL WIGGLESWORTH
Pastour of ye Church of Christ
at Maulden 49 years who
Finished His Work and Entered
Upon an Eternal Sabbath
Of Rest on ye Lord's Day June
ye 10, 1705, in ye 74 year of his age.
Here lyes Interd in Silent Grave Below
Maulden's Physician of Soul and Body two.

There is an allusion to the poem in this epitaph written by Mather, for one of its many editions : —

The Excellent
WIGGLESWORTH.
Remembered by some Good Tokens.
His pen did once Meat from the Eater fetch,
And now he's gone beyond the Eater's reach.
His body once so Thin, was next to None;
From hence he's to Unbodied Spirits flown.
Once his rare skill did all Diseases heal;
And he does nothing now uneasy feel.
He to his Paradise is joyful come ;
And waits with joy to see his Day of Doom.

It was commendable in a parson, and also in anybody, to have more than one profession. The wardens of Christ Church, of

Boston, when writing to London in the year 1759 for an organist, said they wanted "to find a person that understands to play well on an Organ, a Tradesman or a Barber would be most agreeable." They intimated that an organist who could play the barber, or a barber who could play the organ, would have opportunities to shave the congregation; tò quote exactly from their letter,— "the Congregation improving him as they have occasion in his Occupation."

No matter what was the sum of the parson's annual salary, there was but little money in it. It was composed of various materials. A part might be payable "at Boston at some shope there;" a part "in country pay at this towne;" in it were, perhaps, "two pounds of butter for every cow;" a certain weight in meats; "upland winter wheat clean from all trash;" forty cords of firewood. Mr. Lowell says, in one of his published letters, that his great-grandfather, who was minister of Newbury, used to take the grocer's share of his salary in tobacco; and there is a painting still extant representing a meeting of the neighboring clergy, each with his pipe. One day the parson at Easton brought home a bucket of potash and a little black pig which he had received, as his note-book says, on account of "payment for preaching the Gospel." John Eliot, who was known as the Apostle to the Indians, took for a similar account thirty-four pounds' weight of copper pennies and gave this receipt at Roxbury, April 8, 1673: "Received of Colo Williams a Bag of coppers, weight 34 pounds, in part of my salary for the year currant, the same being by estimation £1-13-4 lawful money and for which I am to be accountable." In the year 1751, John Wales, of Raynham, took one third of his salary "in good merchantable iron at £9 per cwt." A part of the salary of Parson Cotton at Pamet was "one ninth part of the drift fish" that came ashore. These drifts were dead or stranded whales, claimed by the town. His majesty's justice of the peace fined a townsman £1 for "lying about a whale" that was probably lying on the shore for the improvement of the parson.

In the year 1747, Edward Pell became the parson of a Cape Cod town, with an annual salary of 135 bushels of corn, 15 bushels of rye, 10 bushels of wheat, and

36 cords of firewood. As he preached for bread without any butter, the poor wife was probably compelled to fire the oven every day to bake the salary; but it did not sustain him for long, as he died in his parish during the year 1752. It was a teaching of the colonial pulpit that the body buried was the identical body to be raised at the general resurrection of the just. This poor grain-fed parson, when dying, thought of that day when the trumpet shall sound and, as the tradition is, he asked his friends to bury his body in the ancient graveyard, because if it should be buried under the pines in the new yard, it "might be overlooked in the resurrection." I feel a touch of pity for this childlike parson. But he might have bethought him of a passage in a sermon of Jonathan Edwards: "There is no hope that God, by reason of the multiplicity of affairs, he hath in mind, will happen to overlook them and not take notice of them when they come to die, and so that their souls shall slip away privately and hide themselves in some secret corner."

The country parson was often struggling against poverty. When William Emerson turned away from his occupation as a schoolmaster and became the parson of Harvard town, he said, "I am too poor to keep a horse." Married five years later, and trying to cultivate the ministry farm, he wrote: "We are poor, and cold, and have little meal, and little wood, and little meat; but, thank God, courage enough." Three years later, the church society in Boston founded by John Cotton wanted him; and the estimation in which he was held appears in the fact that it offered to pay to the town eight hundred dollars, to release him from his lifelong contract. The town refused this offer, but accepted one thousand dollars; and then Parson Emerson with his family moved to Boston, where he found more meal, more wood, and more meat than he had found in his country parish. He said: "The ills of poverty, however, are not so great as those of ecclesiastical dissension."

As a studious man, the parson had but little time for enjoying the society of his family, if he followed the example of Thomas Prince, minister in the Old South meetinghouse of Boston, who wrote the following order of his daily duties: —

"— 1719. Oct. 30. I marry.

Nov. 10. We begin to keep House.

My Proposed Order is

At 5 Get up and go into my Study. Pray and read in the original Bible till 6, and then call up the Family.

At 6½ Go to Family Prayers; and only the Porringer of Chocolat for Breakfast till 7.

At 7 go into my study till 12½, and then do something about House till 1 to Dinner; except on Thursday, study till 10½, then Dress, and at 11 to Lecture.

Dinner at 1.

At 2 Dress and go abroad till candle Light. Except Wednesday, after Dinner, do something about House; Saturday, after Dinner, visit at Dr Sewall's till 2½ and then Home to Study at candle Light and Study to 9½.

At 9½ go to Family Prayers and go to Bed.

N. B. I eat no supper."

As a preacher, the parson was not always remarkable in the estimation of his rural hearers, because many of them stood on a plane below his intellectual level. It has been so ever since those days. Even the celebrated Dean Stanley, of Westminster Abbey, when he preached his first sermon in a country village, was discussed by two old women on their way home after the service, and one of them said : —

"Well, I do feel empty like."

"And so do I," said the other; "that young man did n't give us much to feed on."

The parson was very human. He had his bottle of rum in the study closet, and in the cellar he had many barrels of cider made from his own apples, as was the custom of the times. He believed in the sentiment of Goldsmith's song : —

> "Let schoolmasters puzzle their brains
> With grammar and nonsense and learning,
> Good liquor I stoutly maintain
> Gives genius a better discerning."

He picked up gladly a marriage fee, and sometimes a gift of small value came to his door on New Year's Day. John Emerson, who was settled as parson of the frontier town of Conway in the year 1769, and said of himself that he was "John preaching in the wilderness," kept a diary in which he wrote : —

"January 1st — Had much company. In the evening married a couple. Fee $1.25. Had a cheese given me. Value about $1. Deacon Ware gave a present of beef. Value about 20 cents.

January 4th — Attended to study. Bottle of rum, 50 cents.

January 23d — Married 3 couples. Fee $6.25.

February 4th — Paid a woman taylor for one day, 25 cents. Postage for letters, 17 cents.

May 28th — Set out on horseback for a journey to Boston. The country was in an alarming condition. Some means must be devised to suppress infidelity. Was gone from home near two weeks. Expenses to and from Boston, $2.16.

July 5th — Bottle of rum, 50 cents.

August 1st — Two quarts of rum, $1.50. Paid for killing hog, 17 cents.

October 20th — Put in the cellar for Winter use, 38 barrels of cider."

He sometimes fell into the sinful habits of his people; as did Joseph Penniman, who was dismissed from his parish at Bedford because of drunkenness. He became a farmer in a neighboring town, and was one day summoned to pray for the sick inmates of a house near by. The tradition is that, standing at the top of the stairs, he prayed "the Lord to be very merciful unto Bezaliel who lieth nigh unto death in the north chamber; send thy ministering angels to comfort Bathsheba, groaning with anguish in the south chamber; visit with thy healing grace, Judith, thy sorely afflicted maiden down stairs."[1]

The great day of the parson's life was the day of his ordination. It was a holiday for the town, when fifers and drummers came in from all parts of the county, escorted the procession of councilmen, scholars, particular gentlemen, villagers, and boys into the meeting-house and out of it, and played stirring music to idlers gathered around the whipping-post on the Common. An ordination aroused the drowsy village to a new life, and the expenses of it were cheerfully paid in the tax-rates, although they amounted to more than the parson's salary for a year. When Edwin Jackson was ordained at Woburn, in the year 1729, the town paid for

433 dinners	£54 2 6
178 suppers and breakfasts	8 18 0
Keeping 32 horses 4 days	3 0 0
6 barrels and ½ Cyder	4 11 0
25 Gallons Wine	9 10 0
2 Gallons Brandy and 4 of Rum	1 16 0
Loaf Sugar, lime juice and pipes	1 12 0

A description of the usual events of an ordination is given in the following extract

[1] Nourse, *History of the Town of Harvard.*

from a private letter[1] written by Rev. Lawrence Conant, a member of the ecclesiastical council convened for an ordination at Salem, September 25, 1713: "Your brother Thomas says ye place has grown very much since you lived here and that ye church has got 40 members, who came off from Mr. Noyes' church in Salemtown (13 men and 27 women), and ye town has granted ye Precinct 5 acres of land, and ye Promise of £5 a year for five years, for ye support of ye Gospel in ye Precinct. Ye Church have made choice of ye Reverend Benj. Prescott for their Pastor and have voted him £60 a year and 15 cords of wood for his salary, when single, and £75 when he shall be married. Mr. Prescott is the oldest son of Esquire Jonathan Prescott of Concord and is a promising man about 25 years old, and betrothed to Elizabeth Higginson, a comely daughter of Mr. John Higginson. . . . Ye services in ye meeting house began by read-

[1] For a copy of this letter I am indebted to Mrs. Jane Prescott Townsend, of New Haven, Conn., who is a lineal descendant of Benjamin Prescott, ordained at Salem, Mass., in September, 1713. An extract from the same letter appears on page 48.

ing a part of ye 119th Psalm by Reverend Cotton Mather. After which he read a portion from Thos. Allen's Invitation to Thirsty Sinners. Mr. Hubbard then offered prayer and a Psalm was sung to a most solemn tune, ye oldest deacon reading line by line in solemn voice so that ye whole congregation could join. Mr. Bowers of Beverly next offered a prayer of Ordination and consecration with ye laying on of ye hands of ye elders. Mr. Appleton of Cambridge preached ye sermon from 2nd Cor. 2nd, 16th verse. 'Who is sufficient for these things?' Mr. Shepard gave ye charge and the Rev'd Mr. Greene of ye village ye hand of fellowship and Mr. Gerrish of Wenham made ye concluding prayer. There was an immense concourse of people in ye house, so that every part was crowded and some were on ye beams over ye congregation. Ye Governor was in ye house and His Majesty's Commissioners of ye Customs, and they sat together on a high seat by ye pulpit stairs. Ye Governor appeared very devout and attentive. Although he favors Episcopacy and tolerates ye Quakers and ye Baptists, he is a strong opposer of ye Baptists. He was dressed in a Black velvet coat bordered with gold lace, and puff breeches and gold buckles at ye knees and white stockings. There was a disturbance in ye galleries when it was filled with divers negroes, Mulattoes and Indians, and a negro called Pomp Shorter, belonging to Mr. Gardiner, was called forth and put in ye broad aisle where he was reproved with great awfulness and solemnity. He was then put in ye Deacon's seat, between two Deacons, in view of ye whole Congregation, but ye Sexton was ordered by Prescott to take him out because of his levity and strange contortions of countenance, giving great scandal to ye grave deacons, and put him in the lobby under ye stairs. Some children and a mulatto woman were reprimanded for laughter at Pomp Shorter.

"When ye services at ye house were ended, ye Council and other dignitaries were entertained at ye house of Mr. Epes on the hill near by, and we had a bountiful table with bear's meat and venison, the last was from a fine buck shot in the woods near by. Ye bear was killed in Lynn Woods near Redding. After ye blessing had been craved by Mr. Gerrish of Wenham, word came that ye Buck was shot on the Lord's Day by Pequot, an Indian, who came to Mr. Epes with a lye in his mouth, like Anannias of old. Ye Council thereupon refused to eat of ye venison. But it was afterwards agreed that Pequot should receive 40 stripes save one for lying and profaning the Lord's Day, restore Mr. Epes the cost of the deer and counsiling that a just and righteous sentence on ye sinful Heathen, and as blessing had been craved on ye meat ye Council partook of it except Mr. Shepard whose conscience was tender on ye point of venison."

Notwithstanding some scruples in regard to the venison, it was a jolly ordination dinner, and the thirsty parsons may have "lost sight of decorum;" as Parson Smith, of Falmouth, said concerning the company at the ordination of Samuel Foxcroft in a little town of Maine.[1]

[1] "January 16, 1765, Mr. Foxcroft was ordained at New Gloucester. We had a pleasant journey home. Mr. Longfellow was alert and kept us all merry. A jolly ordination. We lost sight of decorum." — *Diary of Rev. Thomas Smith.*

Dark days in the poor parson's life were apt to come when the jolly ordination had been forgotten, and the humdrum routines of the town had been resumed. Then his relations with parishioners sometimes became disagreeable through no fault of his; and when he suffered from the meanness of those who ruled the parish, he could envy Bunyan's weary pilgrim resting in that "large upper Chamber whose window looked towards the Sun rising" and whose name was Peace. These disagreeable relations usually arose from his salary business. At first it was his duty to collect the salary as it was offered in driblets by the people; and so he went about the parish every week "to gather his own rates." The occupation gave to him an odious name, and the ungodly refused to pay what they called "the Priest's rate." Then the salary was put into the town taxes, and the town undertook the collection of it by a constable. Yet it did not always pay to the poor parson his dues, the temper of the times was so miserly.

John Robinson was ordained at Duxbury in the year 1702. His annual salary was always far in arrear; and at last he was forced to bring a suit against the town to compel a payment. "Well! what do you want now?" said the spokesman of the parish to him; "If we haven't paid up, we gave you the improvement of the island and about thirty acres of upland besides. Isn't that enough without asking for your salary?"

"Ah! yes;" said Mr. Robinson, "you did give me the island. I've mowed it and I don't want a better fence around my cornfield than one windrow of the fodder it cuts. If you should mow that upland you speak of with a razor and rake it with a comb, you wouldn't get enough from it to winter a grasshopper."

After preaching in this parish for thirty-six years, he was still pressing the town to pay the arrears of his salary, when a committee was appointed to make up accounts with him "from the beginning of the world to the present day" — August 7, 1738. Two months later, the following paragraph was written in the town records: —

"Voted that ther meting hous shuld be shot up so that no parson shuld open the same so that Mr. John Robrson of Duxborrough may not get into said meeting hous to preach anay more without orders from the towne."

David Parsons, settled at Leicester in the year 1721, had a violent and long-continued quarrel with the town; and when he was dying, he directed that his body should be buried in his own meadow, which was far away from the churchyard. The grave in the meadow was neglected, its headstone was removed to make a pavement, and eventually it became the cover of an ashes pit, where its inscription declared to the passer-by that the parson "Was laid here October 12, 1743."

In the year 1761, a young man named Joseph Sumner was ordained at Shrewsbury, on a salary of two hundred and forty dollars a year, and he preached in the Shrewsbury meeting-house for the unusual period of sixty-three years. In the latter part of these years, the amount of his salary was cut down one half. Some one asked him, "How do you manage to live and preach on such a small salary?" He replied, in the simplicity of a poor parson, "I have learned that they who have much, have not enough; but those who have little, have no lack." He had the spirit of Archbishop Fénelon, who wrote to a friend, the year before he died, "I ask little from men; I try to render them much, and to expect nothing in return."

When, after forty-one years of service, old age came upon Parson Russell, of Branford, and he was so indisposed as not to come forth on the Sabbath, the town hired as a school-teacher "one who could be helpful in the ministry;" and it asked the invalid to state how much might be deducted from his salary — which was mainly provisions and firewood — for "supplying the pulpit;" or, in other words, for paying the school-teacher. In his reply he wrote: "I conclude you will not think it unreasonable to find me fire wood while I live. As for my yearly salary, you may do just as God may incline your hearts. I leave it wholly with you, depending not on an arm of flesh but on the Living God for my daily bread, and I am not afraid but that He, who feeds the young ravens when they cry, will provide for my support."

> " No gift of comeliness had he, scant grace
> Of bearing, little pride of mien —

> He had the rugged old-time Roundhead face,
> 　Severe and yet serene.
> But through these keen and steadfast eyes of blue
> The soul shone, fearless, modest, strong, and true."

Some eight miles back from Norwich Landing, on the Thames River in Connecticut, there was in colonial times a small hamlet known as West Farms. It is now the town of Franklin. There, in March, 1782, Samuel Nott was "ordained in the ministry" for life, on an annual salary of three hundred and thirty-three dollars and thirty-three cents. In his sixtieth anniversary sermon, which is "most affectionately addressed" to the children, grandchildren, and great-grandchildren of those who invited him "to settle with them in the Gospel Ministry," he reviewed the events of sixty years, and quaintly said, "I have not been kept from the house of God during that long period but eleven Sabbaths; six of them by the lung fever in 1812, and five by breaking a little piece of skin upon the back of my right hand." On the day of this anniversary sermon, the choir sang the same hymns, in the same tunes of "Lenox" and "Stockbridge," that were sung at his ordination sixty years before. It was a pathetic scene. All the members of the ordination choir were dead; all but two old women, seated near the ancient pulpit, who, insensible to the music which they sang before the rose-color of life was blanched, were straining their dull ears to catch the words of the old parson's story.

Then the years came and went, until his life in the parish had extended from the peaceful into the restless state of society, and he was so old that the church desired him to "lay down the ministry in this place;" in other words, they asked him to go. He replied that he was settled for life; and he continued to live and to preach every Sunday, until he was ninety-five years old, when the town induced him to enter into a compromise. His salary was reduced one half, and a colleague was hired at a salary of four hundred dollars a year, which was to be increased to five hundred dollars as soon as the old parson died. He died in the year 1852, ninety-eight years of age; and then was closed the contract made with him in the year 1782. After his death the executor of his estate discovered that he had not received any of the half pay to which he had been entitled. It was demanded from the town, and refused. At last, seeing no chance for an amicable settlement, the executor called to his aid the law. The town offered to settle the debt for one half its amount, and the offer was accepted. So the hereditary Puritan of New England is, like his composite ancestor, as "penurious as the last drips of a washerwoman's wringing."

XII.

THE NOTORIOUS MINISTERS.

VERY different from the poor parsons were the notorious ministers. There was one in the colonial meeting-house whose name was Samuel Parris. He was in Harvard College awhile; then he was in commercial business in the West Indies; then, being forty years old, he drifted into the pulpit of the meeting-house of Salem Village. Here his nature developed itself in an artful quarrel with his congregation about a piece of land. On Sunday, the 27th day of March, 1692, he wrote in his church book: "The Devil hath been raised amongst us and his rage is Vehement and terrible, and when he shall be silenced the Lord only knows." Researches into the events of his time have disclosed the fact that the Vehement Devil to whom he referred was none other than himself. He had taken hints from Cotton Mather, another notorious minister, whose writings had created in the public mind a passion for anything that appeared to be marvelous, supernatural, and diabolical. Mather was then thirty years old; a man of talent, who exercised a large influence on the theology and politics of the times, and a minister with his father in the North meeting-house of Boston. With this enthusiast as an inspirer, Parris started a witchcraft conspiracy in the year 1692, which made the greatest blot on the pages of New England's history.

His tools were three children, Elizabeth Parris, his daughter, nine years old; Abigail Williams, his niece, eleven years old; and Ann Putnam, twelve years old, a daughter of the parish clerk. These children had heard the marvelous witchcraft stories published by the Mathers, and they were seized with such a frantic interest in them that they held meetings to study and perform some of the witcheries described. They practiced grotesque postures, unnatural outcries, dumbness, convulsions and cramps of the body. When they had perfected themselves in these actions, they played them off for the first time, in the meeting-house, on the Sunday when Parris wrote in his church book that a Vehement Devil hath been raised. Deodate Lawson, a believer in witchcraft, preached for Parris that day. After a psalm had been sung, Abigail Williams cried out, "Stand up now and name your text!" Ann Putnam shouted to him, "There's a yellow bird on your hat; it hangs on the pin of the pulpit!" After he had begun his sermon, another called to him, "Now, there's enough of that!" The people were alarmed, for in their belief it was the devil who spoke with the tongues of the "afflicted children," as they were called. The Mathers had portrayed the devil as a black man, who carried a red book and a pen, soliciting subscribers to his service, whispering in your ear and standing behind to prompt your speech. Physicians who examined the children were perplexed, but finally declared that they were bewitched. Then the inquiry was, who are the witches that have bewitched them? The children refused to answer; but finding it impossible to escape the earnest inquiry, except by confessing their own fraud (which they did confess in after years), they gave the names of three persons; and thereafter these children, under the control of Parris, became the chief witch-finders for the Salem tragedy. This was the beginning of it. Its result was the imprisonment of more than a hundred and fifty men and women, and the murder of twenty who were "as innocent in their lives as they were heroic in their deaths."

The extravagant superstition of Cotton Mather appears in his description of the passing of the first victim, Bridget Bishop, to the gallows. He says, "She gave a look towards the great and spacious meeting-house and a Demon invisibly entering the house tore down a part of it." The truth probably was, that a partition or floor had yielded to the pressure of the crowd of astonished spectators. This notorious minister was now in his element. During the summer of 1692, he with Parris and others caused to be reproduced in Salem Village, which is now the town of Danvers, all the horrors of the Inquisition of Torquemada.

They had Puritan laws to support their acts. The original laws of the Massachusetts colony said: "If any man or woman be a witch, that is hath, or consulted with, a familiar spirit, they shall be put to death." A law of the Plymouth colony, enacted in the year 1636, declared "solemn compaction or conversing with the Divell by way of witchcraft, conjuration, or the like," to be "capitall offences lyable to death." To avoid trouble with Indian wizards, this law was revised in the year 1671, so as to touch English people only. It said: "If any Christian, so called, be a Witch, that is hath, or consulteth with, a familiar Spirit, he or she shall be put to death." These laws were in force during the year 1692 by authority of the province legislature; but they were not in touch with the new colonial life. Like a heap of dry bones, they belonged to the past.

Witchcraft has existed in all times; and it exists to-day in those who are known to us as conjurers, necromancers, legerdemainists, clairvoyants, fortune-tellers, and mediums of spiritualism. These all are consulters of "a familiar spirit." Their highest grade is seen in a hereditary caste of India which has made jugglery a fine art, and which caused the Emperor Jehangeer to believe that he saw a Hindu throw a rope into the air, run up it, and disappear into space. Their lowest grade is seen in wrinkled hags, "with viper's eyes and weamy wimy voices," who thrive on their repute as witches in rural towns of Old England and perhaps also of New England; whose principal business is with love affairs. A rustic maid discovers that her lover is false; she seeks advice from the village witch, and, acting upon it, she buys a sheep's heart, sticks it full of pins, and roasts it over a quick fire while three times calling her lover by name to return. Then she says the Lord's Prayer, goes backward upstairs to her chamber, and the charm which is to bring back her lover is completed. "That wer all owin to thickwitch," said a Somersetshire rustic, whose pig had suddenly died; "an' as sure as thee sits in thick chair be it true theus witches have the power ter kill our animals an' ter make our loives mizerubble. They do kip red books an' funny letters in 'em an' freames wi' nurruh picters in 'em, an' tooads oo dozins ov 'em, and hoss shus, an' all zoorts o' queer things ver charmin' a peepel." Persons called witches were hung in Scotland a hundred years before the Salem tragedy, for causing iron pots, firlots, and sieves to skip about. The trick was done by strings fastened to these things and passed out of a window for a confederate to pull; as is explained in Reginald Scot's "Discovery of Witchcraft," printed in the year 1582. At that time, Andrew Duncan, minister of Crail in Scotland, was protesting against the cruel tortures practiced by a neighboring proprietor upon an old woman who was called a witch; saying that "according to the ordinance of the Presbytrie, he had tane Geillis Gray, suspect of witchcraft, whom the Laird of Lathocker tuick from him, and carreit hir to his place of Lathocker and their torturit hir, whairby now scho is become impotent and may not labour for hir living as scho wes wont." [1]

The witchcraft court was a special commission appointed by Sir William Phips, the fresh governor of the province, apparently on motion of his intimate friends Increase and Cotton Mather. He describes how it happened in a letter written to London: "When I first arrived I found this Prov-

[1] Beveridge, *The Churchyard Memorials of Crail.*

ince miserably harassed with a most horrible witchcraft or possession of devils. . . . some scores of poor people were taken with preternatural torments, some scalded with brimstone, some had pins stuck in their flesh, others hurried into fire and water and some dragged out of their houses and carried over the tops of trees and hills for many miles together." Of course this ridiculous sketch of the condition of New England society was dictated for the governor by Cotton Mather. It was a repetition of his own stories. Consequently, the governor was prevailed upon, he says, " to give a Commission of Oyer and Terminer for discovering what Witchcraft might be at the bottom."

All the victims of this court were condemned on spectral evidence. One of the " afflicted children " would testify that she saw and felt the spectre of the accused person; that it tormented her and she struck at it. A corresponding bruise was found on the body of the accused, or a rent was found in its garments. As everybody wore the same clothing continuously until worn out, it was easy to find rents in anybody's garments. Cotton Mather, writing to his friend

John Richards, one of the judges, said that when he finds any bruises or rents inflicted by the spectral hands of the accused: "Hold them for you have catched a Witch."

The court was not a picturesque tribunal, composed of noted lawyers met to tender their advice on an important question of government. It was composed of nine men, not one of whom had received an education in law; two had been educated for the ministry, two were physicians, others were tradesmen and yeomen; and one of the appointees declined to have anything to do with the business. Five of them constituted a quorum for trials; one of the five being always John Richards, a friend and parishioner of Cotton Mather. Their chief was Stoughton, deputy governor of the province, noted as an obstinate, malignant, and passionate man. They held their sessions at intervals in a dilapidated meeting-house, whose broken windows, covered here and there by boards, were typical of the darkened condition of their minds. They made no concealment of an intention to condemn all prisoners brought to the bar who refused to confess that they were witches.

No counsel was allowed to the accused; execution followed quick upon judgment.

When Rebecca Nourse, seventy years old and eminent for her piety, was tried as a witch by these men, she was so hard of hearing and so full of grief that she could not understand all that was said against her, and no pains were taken that she should hear. The "afflicted children" made hidden outcries when the jury brought in a verdict of not guilty, and Stoughton sent them back to change their verdict. Then he condemned her to death. To prepare for this fate, she was taken from prison to the meeting-house on the communion Sunday before she was to be executed, and was there excommunicated from the church of Christ, so far as it could be done by a notorious minister whose name was Nicholas Noyes.

One of the conspicuous victims was the Rev. George Burroughs, who had been for three years, from 1680 to 1683, the minister of Salem Village, and in the year 1689, a rival of Parris as a candidate for the same pulpit. He was now minister of the town of Wells, in Maine. He was a man of large stature and great strength, and it was known that he could easily lift a barrel of molasses or cider, and carry it ashore from a canoe. Cotton Mather said these were "such feats of strength as could not be done without diabolical assistance." He was executed, and his body, when taken from the gallows, was thrown into a hole, without any pretense of a burial.

Another conspicuous victim was Giles Corey, a respectable citizen, eighty years old. When he was brought, as a witch, before the court, he pleaded not guilty; but he would not put himself on trial by the jury because, as Calef says, "they having cleared none upon trial, and knowing there would be the same witnesses against him, rather chose to undergo what death they would put him to." He was stretched naked upon the ground, on his back, and iron was laid upon him, "as much as he could bear and more." Under this slow process of torture his tongue was pressed out of his mouth, and the sheriff with his cane forced it in when he was dying.

It seems incredible that there was a population of respectable white men in New England who could look upon these atrocious travesties of justice without rising up and driving the Salem judges and ministers into the sea. The spirit of Christianity prohibits torture; but Giles Corey was tortured in the name of it, and by magistrates whose hearts were so callous that they exulted in the sufferings of every victim. The practice of such cruelties in an English community would be impossible now, because, since Puritanism died, a new moral sense has been born in man which teaches him that there is a sacredness in human life, and causes him to shrink from inflicting pain for pain's sake. It does not palliate the cruelty of these men of 1692, to say that they are to be judged by the light which they had. They had light enough, both in reason and revelation, as some of them in after time confessed. They knew that a part of the community was opposed to their acts. Thomas Brattle wrote, at the time: "Although the chief judge and some of the other judges be very zealous for these proceedings, yet this you may take for truth; that there are several about the Bay, men for understanding, judgment and piety, inferior to few, if any, in New England, who do utterly condemn the said proceedings."

These were compelled to keep silence, for the theocratic tyranny which ruled over the province made it unsafe for honest men to express their opinions in public. All were in fear of being accused of witchcraft, and many sought for safety by flight into New Hampshire and New York. The promoters of the Salem tragedy were like the rulers who threw Christian men and woman to lions, in order "to make a Roman holiday;" like those who burned at the stake the martyrs of Smithfield; like those who in France broke criminals on the wheel a hundred years ago; like those on the Danube who, in recent years, have impaled their foes. Under the rule of its theocracy New England had become one of the dark places of the earth, "full of the habitations of cruelty."

At last the court was suddenly stopped by the governor, who said that he "found many persons in a strange ferment of dissatisfaction which was increased by some hot spirits that blew up the flame . . . that the Devil had taken upon him the name and shape of several persons who were doubtless innocent." In fact, the conspirators had begun to accuse as witches some of the Boston ministers, but not Cotton Mather, although, as he himself complained, he was considered to be the " doer of all hard things that were done in the prosecution of the witchcraft."

The first sign of a recovery from the horrible delusion was a proposition made in October, 1692, for a day of fasting. A " Committee of Religion " was chosen in the House of Representatives, and a declaration enumerating " Sundry Evils to be confessed " was drafted. This paper, which is still preserved in the archives of Massachusetts, is in the handwriting of Cotton Mather, who was alert to put himself on the right side of the fence in case there should be a popular uprising. Among other things he said : —

" Wicked Sorceries have been practiced in the land ; and, in the late inexplicable storms from the Invisible world thereby brought upon us, wee were left, by the Just Hand of Heaven unto those Errors whereby Great Hardships were brought upon Innocent persons, and (wee feare) Guilt incurr'd, which wee have all cause to bewayl, with much confusion of o^r Face before the Lord."

When he wrote that, was he thinking of George Burroughs, and Rebecca Nourse, and Giles Corey, and seventeen other victims as "innocent persons"? He had stigmatized them in print as "a fearful knot of proud, forward, ignorant, envious, and malicious creatures — a Witch gang!"

The governor and council rejected the declaration written by Cotton Mather, and the matter remained for some time in suspense. At last it was acknowledged that a Fast was necessary to appease the divine wrath, under which Massachusetts had suffered in many of its enterprises because, as was generally believed, of the errors committed in the witch trials; and they accepted a declaration drawn by Samuel Sewall, who had been one of the judges at Salem. Whittier has sketched the figure of this noted man in a few lines : —

> "I hear the tap of the elder's cane,
> And his awful periwig I see,
> And the silver buckles of shoe and knee.
> Stately and slow, with thoughtful air,
> His black cap hiding his whitened hair,
> Walks the Judge of the Great Assize,
> Samuel Sewall."

The proclamation was published in December, 1696; reciting many reasons, it commanded, "That Thursday the Fourteenth of January next be observed as a Day of Prayer with Fasting. . . . That so all God's people may offer up fervent Supplications unto him. . . . That he would show us what we know not, and help us wherein we have done amiss, to doe so no more, . . . especially that whatever Mistakes, on either hand, have been fallen into, either by the body of this People, or any Orders of Men, referring to the last Tragedie raised amongst us by Satan and his Instruments, through the awfull Judgment of God; He would humble us therefore, and pardon all the Errors of his Servants and People."

That day revealed a ray of light in the general darkness. It marked a halo around Samuel Sewall. He rises in his pew in the Old South meeting-house and hands to the minister, as he passes by on his way to the pulpit, a written confession of his repentance for the part he had taken in the witch trials. He stands up during the reading of his confession to the congregation, and he silently bows his head when the reading is ended. It is said that, during the remainder of his life, he observed this fast day privately on each annual return of it.

> "All the day long, from dawn to dawn,
> His door was bolted, his curtain drawn;
> No foot on his silent threshold trod,
> No eye looked on him save that of God,
> As he baffled the ghosts of the dead with charms
> Of penitent tears, and prayers, and psalms,
> And, with precious proofs from the sacred word
> Of the boundless pity and love of the Lord,
> His faith confirmed and his trust renewed
> That the sin of his ignorance, sorely rued,
> Might be washed away in the mingled flood
> Of his human sorrow and Christ's dear blood."

The twelve jurymen of the witch court also repented and published a confession of their errors. They said: "We ourselves were not capable to understand, nor able to withstand, the mysterious delusions of the powers of darkness and prince of the air; but were, for want of knowledge in ourselves and better information from others, prevailed with to take up with such evidence against the accused as, on further consideration and better information we justly fear was insufficient for the touching the lives of any. . . . We do declare we would none of us do such things again on such grounds for the whole world."

Nicholas Noyes repented, and caused to be blotted from his church records the excommunication of Rebecca Nourse. Samuel Parris repented not. After a long struggle he was driven out from Salem; he drifted away into Connecticut, and there he disappeared from public view. The last mention of him that I have found appears in an advertisement, published in the Boston "Weekly News-Letter," the 24th of June, 1731; inquiring for "Any Person or Persons who knew Mr. Samuel Parris, formerly of Barbadoes, afterwards of Boston, in New England, Merchant, and after that Minister of Salem Village etc., deceased."

As to the reverend Mr. Cotton Mather, he never made a confession, nor did he show any signs of repentance. On the contrary, he set himself to create a witchcraft excitement in Boston, for he needed an illustration to justify his acts at Salem. He took in charge a young wench named Margaret Rule, who lived not far from his house in Hanover Street, and had been, as he said, "assaulted by eight cruel spectres;" which "brought unto her a book about a cubit long, — a red book and thick, but not very broad, — and they demanded of her that she would set her hand to that book as a sign of her becoming a servant of the Devil." From the day of this assault, he said, "until the ninth day following she kept an entire fast, and yet she was to all appearances as fresh, as lively, as hearty, at the nine days' end as before they began. . . . Her tormentors permitted her to swallow a mouthful of somewhat that might increase her miseries, whereof a spoonful of Rum was the most considerable."

This wizard show was noised through the town, and many people came to see it. Let us go in for a moment. We ascend to her chamber, which is dimly lighted with candles, and find about thirty persons present. Increase Mather is sitting on a stool near the head of the bed. His son Cotton Mather sits on the bedside, and says to the woman in bed : —

"Margaret, do there a great many witches sit upon you?"

"Yes," she replies, and then she falls into a fit. He places his hand upon her face, brushes it with his glove; then he rubs her stomach. She now revives. He asks her:—

"Don't you know there is a hard master?"

"Yes."

"Do you believe?"

She falls into a fit, and he rubs her breast, when she revives again.

Increase Mather now inquires if she knows who the spectres are. She knows, but she will not tell. Then Cotton Mather says to her: "You have seen the black man, have you not?"

"No."

"The brushing of you gives you ease, don't it?"

"Yes." She then turns herself and groans and Cotton Mather says:—

"Now the witches scratch you, and bite you, and pinch you; don't they?"

"Yes."

Increase Mather prays for half an hour, chiefly against the power of the Devil, and witchcraft, and that God would bring out the afflictors. During the prayer Cotton Mather rubs Margaret and brushes her as before. After the Amen, he asks her:—

"You did not hear when we were at prayer, did you?"

"Yes."

"You don't always hear?"

"No."

Turning about to an attendant, he asks: "What does she eat and drink?" The answer is:—

"She does not eat at all, but drinks Rum."

This happened in September, 1693, and is a fact of recorded history. In the January following, Cotton Mather was handing about the town written certificates signed by eight men (it will be remembered that she was "assaulted by eight spectres"), who declared that they had seen Margaret Rule, "in her afflictions from the invisible world, lifted up from her bed by an invisible force so as to touch the garret floor, while yet neither her feet nor any other part of her body rested either on the bed or any support; and it was as much as several of us could do, with all our strength, to pull her down."

Here, evidently, was a trick which has long been practiced by magicians in India. A recent writer mentions it as he saw it: "A woman seeming to defy the laws of gravitation, sitting two feet from the ground, in open sunlight, with her wrist on the hilt of an ordinary sword. It is possible," he says, "that she was sitting in a loop of wire attached to the sword hilt." Mr. Andrew Lang speaks of having seen a similar trick. He says: "The suspended woman was examined by an English officer well known to me and by the surgeon of his regiment, who could find no wire. She had been mesmerized and was rigid. On the other hand," he says, "a suspended man was exhibited before the governor of an East Indian Presidency whose aid-de-camp made a rush and found a wire."

The curtain falls on the farce of Cotton Mather and the Tipsy Wench. His imposture is exposed; many of the notorious ministers stand by him for a while; but the community distrusts him ever afterward. In subsequent years the reality of his position had become so apparent to him that his record of it excites tender emotions in a reader of his diary. In this he wrote: —

— " Some, on purpose to affront me, call their negroes by the name of Cotton Mather, that so they may with some shadow of truth assert crimes as committed by one of that name, which the hearers take to be Me."

— "Where is the man whom the female sex have spit more of their venom at?"

— "Where is the man who has been so tormented with such monstrous relatives?"

— "There is not a man in the world so reviled, so slandered, so cursed among sailors."

— "The College for ever puts all possible marks of disesteem upon me."

— "My company is as little sought for, and there is as little resort unto it as any minister that I am acquainted with."

— "And many look on me as the greatest sinner."

Public opinion was soon turned against all witchcrafts, and became willing to listen to the sad cries of the children of those who had suffered; their estates having been ruined and their families impoverished. On the 3d day of November, 1709, Cotton Mather, always ready to catch a favoring tide, appeared with a sermon on the subject which he preached to the legislature; speaking as if he had been innocent of all connection with the Salem tragedy, he said:—

"In two or three too Memorable Days of Temptation that have been upon us, there have been Errors committed. You are always ready to Declare unto all the World, That you Disapprove those Errors. You are willing to inform all Mankind with your declarations: That Persons are not to be judg'd with confederates with Evil Spirits meerly because the Evil Spirits do make Possessed People cry out upon them.

"Could any thing be proposed further, by way of Reparation, Besides the General Day of Humiliation, which was appointed and observed thro' the Province, to bewayl the Errors of our Dark time, some years ago: You would be willing to hearken to it."

They did hearken; but no reparation was ever made to the heirs of those who had suffered death at Salem. At various times petitions on their behalf were sent to the General Court, and these were followed by petitions to reward the heirs of Cotton Mather. For example: on the 8th day of December, 1738, the House of Representatives appointed a committee "to get the best Information they can in the circumstances of the persons and families who suffered in the Calamity of the times in and about the year 1692."

Four days after this, there was presented

to the House a petition of Samuel Mather, son of Cotton Mather,

"Setting forth the publick and eminent Services of his venerable and honoured Grandfather and Father in the Cause and Interest of the Province in many Instances and on Divers Occasions, as particularly therein enumerated, both in civil and religious respects, praying this Court would please to make him an allowance for the said Services."

A petition on behalf of Cotton Mather's sisters was presented from the same source, December 20th; and still another from the son, on the 22d of June, 1739; praying for consideration

"On Account of the public and extraordinary Services of his Ancestors, as entered the 12th and 20th of December last; and a Petition of Maria Fifield, Elizabeth Byles, and others, Heirs of Dr. Increase Mather, praying the Consideration of the Court on account of their Father's publick Services."

The record says that the question was put to the House, "Whether any Grant shall be made the Petitioners? It passed in the Negative, and Ordered That the Petitions be dismissed." Nothing was done for the

Mather heirs; and as they stood in the way of a reparation due to others, nothing was done for the heirs of the witchcraft victims.

Cotton Mather's diaries, which are preserved as curiosities in antiquarian libraries, speak his own indictment against himself. They show, first of all, that he was a crafty politician; that as a minister, he was infallible in his own eyes, cherished an immense value of his own importance, and claimed a personal influence with the Supreme Being. He boasted that his prayers were rewarded by visions of white-robed angels, from whose lips he received assurances of divine favor. You may see in his own handwriting an account of his interview with an angel of God. It is written in the Latin tongue, and on the margin of the page he gives his reason for concealing the record in a dead language: "Hæc scribo Latine, ne cara mea conjux has chartas aliquando inspiciens intelligat," which, being translated, is, "I write this in Latin so that my dear wife, should she inspect these pages, may not understand them." He talked of ghosts that entered his study and carried away his manuscripts; for he believed that

> "The spiritual world
> Lies all about us, and its avenues
> Are open to the unseen feet of phantoms
> That come and go."

His third wife, and "unaccountable consort," as he called her, Lydia Lee, daughter of a clergyman and widow of a Boston merchant, did not know what to make of him; and some historians have suffered in the same perplexity. The last biographer [1] would palliate his witchcraft intoxications by a new theory, which is stated thus: —

"I am much disposed to think that necromancers, witches, mediums — what not — actually do perceive in the infinite realities about us things that are imperceptible to normal beings; but that they perceive them only at a sacrifice of their higher faculties — mental and moral — not inaptly symbolized in the old tales of those who sell their souls. . . . Are we not to-day beginning to guess that there may be in heaven and earth more things than are yet dreamt of in your philosophy?"

The common sense of the English race can perceive no witcheries "in the infinite realities about us," nor is it inclined to make any philosophic guesses about the character

[1] Wendell, *Cotton Mather, The Puritan Priest.* 1891.

of Cotton Mather. He made a great deal of noise and did a great deal of harm, but there is nothing left of him now save a handful of dust in the tomb on Copp's Hill where he was buried in the year 1727. The loungers who dwell in neighboring streets, and who are sitting on the same benches every summer day, within the inclosure of the hill, gossiping, sewing, or spelling out for their children the quaint inscriptions on the surrounding stones, point to his tomb as to a relic about which there is some mysterious notoriety. But those who are familiar with the events of his times cannot look upon it without being reminded of another scene. It is at Salem, on the 19th day August, 1692; he is mounted on a horse standing at the foot of the gallows on which hangs George Burroughs, who had been a minister of the gospel for twenty years; he points to the lifeless body swinging in the air, and harangues the spectators, telling them that this murdered clergyman was not an ordained minister, but a witch; assuring them that "the Devil has often been transformed into an angel of light."

XIII.

THE SIMPLE EVANGELIST.

COTTON Mather had been under the sod thirteen years when Whitefield appeared in Boston. The difference between the two preachers was as between night and morning. He was then a young man, just scant of twenty-six years, in whose favor were a homely countenance, a melodious voice, an eloquent tongue, a graceful manner, and the repute of a blameless life. He had graduated at Oxford, was a priest of the Church of England, and a missionary evangelist whose sermons were a call to immediate repentance. His method of setting forth religious truths was a novelty; and therefore no preacher, apostle, or prophet was ever surrounded by audiences so enormous as those which congregated whenever he preached, whether on week-days or Sundays. They overflowed from the meeting-house into the highway; from the highway into the fields. His fame had preceded him. A letter dated at Boston, October 22, 1740, says: "I perceive you were impatient to know what kind of an introduction he had among us. We (ministers, rulers and people) generally received him as an angel of God. When he preached his farewell sermon on our Common there were twenty-three thousand hearers at a moderate computation. . . . Such a power and presence of God with a preacher, and in religious assemblies, I never saw before. . . . Mr. Whitefield has not a warmer friend anywhere than the first man among us. Our Governor has showed him the highest respect, carried him in his coach from place to place, and could not help following him fifty miles out of town."

John Wesley said of Whitefield's first visit to Boston: " While he was here and in the neighboring places he was extremely weak in body. Yet the multitudes of hearers were so great, and the effects wrought on them so astonishing, as the oldest men then alive in the town had never seen before."

He came at a time appropriate to his work; when a chilling system of religion preached in the colonial meeting-house had stunted the moral and intellectual growth of New England as east winds have stunted the pines of Cape Cod. A majority of the people had become so degenerate that they were exemplifying the "total depravity" of the human race. Conventions of ministers declared that there had been a "great and visible decay of piety" in the churches. A memorial to the General Court of Massachusetts, May 30, 1694, "By Many Ministers of ye Gospel then meeting in Boston," described a condition of sin and iniquity existing in New England not unlike that which prevailed in Pompeii when Vesuvius overwhelmed it with ashes.

All this was a reflection and echo of a similar condition of society existing in Old England; where, from the beginning to the middle of the eighteenth century, drunkenness, licentiousness, infidelity as to religion, were the characteristics of all classes. In the year 1710, Mary Wortley wrote that there were "more atheists among the fine ladies than among the lowest rakes." Montesquieu, who visited England in the year 1729, said that there was no religion at all there, "if anybody spoke of it, everybody laughed;" and in the year 1738, Bishop Secker was saying: "In this we cannot be mistaken — that open and professed disregard of religion is become the distinguishing character of the age." When Sir Robert Walpole was prime minister, it was a well-relished jest in London that he was to introduce to Parliament a bill to erase the word "not" from the Commandments and to insert it in the Creed. This jest represented the character of English society on both sides of the Atlantic.

It was to such a people that Whitefield came to preach the gospel when no other preacher could awaken attention. He played on his audiences as if they were a musical instrument from which he could evoke many tones. The histrionic art was born in him, but it was refined by a tender sincerity which convinced his hearers that he was speaking to them words of truth. They eagerly listened, and

> "The scoffing tongue was prayerful,
>   And the blinded eyes found sight,
> And hearts, as flint aforetime,
>   Grew soft in his warmth and light."

The wonderful effects of his preaching were due, not only to the state of the times, but to his personal qualifications for the work, and to a voice and manner that captivated the attention of all hearers. His voice, as Franklin said, produced the pleasure given by beautiful music, and so perfect was its articulation that it could be heard easily by a congregation of thirty thousand people. Sometimes he wept while speaking; sometimes he paused exhausted by emotion. In one of his sermons he addresses an attendant angel, whom he has portrayed as about to ascend from the congregation to carry a report to the Eternal Throne. He stamps with his foot, lifts his hands and eyes to Heaven, and exclaims, "Stop, Gabriel! Stop, Gabriel! Stop, ere you enter the sacred portals, and carry with you the news of one sinner converted to God!" This apostrophe to an imaginary messenger, which in emotionless print may appear to be ludicrous, was accompanied with such natural and eloquent action that the historian Hume said it surpassed anything he had ever heard from the pulpit. In the course of another sermon he exclaims, "Look yonder! What is that I see?" Then he describes, in all its details, the agony in the Garden of Gethsemane, and he makes its sad scenes so plainly visible that the eyes of the congregation are wet with sympathetic tears. Southey said of him: "Sometimes at the close of a sermon he would personate a judge about to perform the last awful part of his office. With eyes full of tears, and an emotion that made his speech falter, after a pause which kept the whole audience in breathless expectation of what was to come, he would proceed: 'I am now going to put on my condemning cap! Sinner! I must do it; I must pronounce sentence upon you!' And then in a tremendous strain of eloquence describing the eternal punishment of the wicked, he recited the words of Christ: 'Depart from me, ye cursed, into everlasting fire, prepared for the Devil and his angels.'"

His sermons were spoken without reference to any manuscript; and the reader of the printed copies finds nothing in them of that power of eloquence by which he swayed the repentant multitude. But let us listen to his sincere words. He is preaching from the text, "The Lord shall be thine everlasting light." The Brattle Street meeting-house in Boston is thronged with listeners. They fill the seats, the aisles, the doorways, and the windows. He is half through the sermon as we push ourselves in; and we can see that no sluggard-waker is needed to keep the audience awake, nor any inspectors of youth to keep wretched boys in order: —

. . . "Jesus Christ the Sun of Righteousness shall be what the sun is to the visible world; that is, the light and life of his people. I say all the people of God. You see now the sun shines on us all. I never heard that the sun said, 'Lord, I will not shine on the Presbyterians, I will not shine on the Independents, I will not shine on the people called Methodists, those great enthusiasts.' The sun never said, 'I will not shine on the Papists;' the sun shines on all; which shows that Jesus Christ's love is open to all that are made willing by the Holy Ghost to accept of him. And, therefore, it is said: 'The sun of Righteousness shall arise with healing in his wings.' If you were all up this morning before the sun arose at 5 o'clock, how beautiful was his first appearance! How pleasant to behold the flowers opening to the rising sun! I appeal to you, yourselves, when you were looking out of the window, or walking about, or opening your shop, if in a spiritual frame, whether you did not say: 'Arise, thou sun of Righteousness, with healing under thy wings, on me!' All that the natural sun is to the world, Jesus Christ is, and more, to his people. Without the sun we should have no corn, or fruit of any kind. What a dark place the world would be without the sun; and how dark the world would be without Jesus Christ! And as the sun does really communicate its rays to the earth, the plants, and all the lower creation, so the Son of God does really communicate his life and power to every new created soul. . . . How many thousand things are there that make you mourn here below! Who can tell the tears that godly parents shed for ungodly children! O, you young folks, you do not know what plagues your children may be to you! O, they are pretty things while young, like rattlesnakes and alligators which I have seen when little and beautiful; but put them in your bosom, and you will find that they are dangerous. How many there are in the world that would wish, if it were lawful, that God had written them childless! There is many a poor creature that makes his father's heart ache. I once asked a godly widow, 'Madam, how is your son?' She turned aside with tears, and said, 'Sir, he is no son to me now.' What, in the world, can come up to that! . . . When I was in Bristol, I could not help remembering good Mr. Middleton who used to have the gout very much, and in that closet were kept his crutches. Now, thought I, he needs them no more; the days of his mourning are ended. And so shall ours be, by and by, too; when we shall no longer want our spiritual crutches or armor, but shall say to the helmet of hope, the shield of faith, I have no more need of thee. Then the all prevailing weapon of prayer shall be changed into songs of praise; when God himself shall be our everlasting light; a sun that shall never go down more, but shall beam forth his infinite and eternal love in a beatific state forever."

It is related that a man who stood listening to Whitefield, at Exeter, held a stone in his hand which he intended to throw at the preacher. As he listened the stone dropped from his hand; and after the sermon he went up and said: "Mr. Whitefield, I came here to break your head, but God has broken my heart." A ship-builder, who was asked what he thought of him, replied: "When I go to my parish church I can build a ship from stem to stern, under the Parson's sermon; but when I hear Mr. Whitefield preach I can't lay a single plank, were it to save my soul." 'Benjamin Franklin, who heard Whitefield preach at Philadelphia, said: "I perceived he intended to finish with a collection, and I silently resolved he should get nothing from me. I had in my pocket a handful of copper money, three or four silver dollars, and five pistoles in gold. As he proceeded I began to soften and concluded to give the copper; another stroke of his oratory made me ashamed of that, and I determined to give the silver; and he finished so admirably that I emptied my pocket into the collector's dish, gold and all."

The results produced by Whitefield's preaching in New England have been diversely interpreted. A letter dated at Boston, in December, 1740, says: "His visit here will be esteemed a distinguished mercy of heaven by many. A small set of gentlemen amongst us, when they saw the affections of the people so moved under his preaching, would attribute it only to his force of voice and gesture. But the impressions on many are so lasting and have been so transforming as to carry plain signatures of a divine hand going along with them." A letter from a country minister, printed in March, 1744, says that in consequence of Whitefield's preaching, "the Bible hath appeared to some to be a new book and the Catechism of the Assembly of Divines to be a new and most excellent Composure, though before they saw no great Excellency to be in the one or the other." A convention of hard-shell ministers, at Boston, spoke of the result as "The late Errors in Doctrine and Disorders in Practice," and they printed a pamphlet condemning it; while another convention of ministers spoke of it as "The late happy Revival of Religion."

Whitefield returned to England, where he preached as he had preached in the colonies. On a second visit to New England, in the year 1744, he found that some ministers had changed their attitude towards him. He had done what they could not do. Therefore they sympathized with the Faculty of Harvard College, which issued what was called a Testimony against him as an enthusiast, or "one that acts either according to dreams or some sudden impulses and impressions upon his mind, which he fondly imagines to be from the Spirit of God. . . . We think it our duty," said the Faculty, "to bear our strongest testimony against that itinerant way of preaching which this gentleman was the first promoter of amongst us, and still delights to continue in." Yale College, by its Faculty, acted in the same manner.

Thaddeus Maccarty, minister of Kingston, near Plymouth, accepted Whitefield's teaching and was compelled to quit his pulpit. As soon as he had gone, the town appointed a committee of eight men "to prevent itinerant preachers from disturbing the peace of the town." The selectmen of Duxbury were directed to take "care of the meeting house to keep out itinerant preachers," who, like Whitefield, were preachers of the simple gospel. At Worcester, where Whitefield preached to crowds gathered by the acre under the open sky, it was voted to be an offense if any member of the church "shall hereafter countenance itinerant preaching."

After Whitefield had gone, James Davenport, the minister of Southold, on Long Island, started on a hunt for unconverted ministers, and he went through county parishes warning people of their danger in following the guidance of such shepherds. In reaching Boston he was arrested and tried for uttering "many slanderous and reviling speeches against godly and faithful ministers." The verdict was "Not guilty," but a result of all these matters was a deep commotion in the minds of the people on the question, Who is and who is not converted. There were reasons for believing that some preachers in the colonial meeting-house were not converted men, before the Great Awakening of the year 1740 began its course. Whitefield wrote in his diary : "I insisted on the doctrine of the new birth, and also on the necessity of a minister being converted before he could preach aright. . . . The Spirit of the Lord enabled me to speak with such vigor against sending unconverted men into the ministry, that two ministers, with tears in their eyes, publicly confessed that they had lain hands on two young men without so much as asking them whether they were born again of God or not."

When Whitefield was preaching at Newburyport, a stone was thrown at him as he stood on the meeting-house steps, before an audience that filled High Street. It struck the Bible which he held in his hand. Lifting up the book, he said: "I have a warrant from God to preach the Gospel; his seal is in my hand, and I stand in the King's highway." He died suddenly in that town, in the year 1770. On the 2d day of October, at one o'clock of the afternoon, all the bells of Newburyport were tolled, and the flags of all vessels in the harbor were flying at half-mast. At two o'clock, the bells were tolled again; at three o'clock, the solemn knell was rung, and the procession of mourners, a mile in length, walked to the meeting-house. There the funeral services were conducted in presence of a thronged assembly, and many persons stood in mournful silence without. They sang the hymn by Dr. Watts, "Why do we mourn departing friends?" then they buried him under the pulpit, and his memory now hallows the ancient town. Whittier says: —

> "Under the church of Federal Street,
> Under the tread of its Sabbath feet,
> Walled about by its basement stones,
> Lie the marvellous preacher's bones.
> No saintly honors to them are shown,
> No sign nor miracle have they known;
> But he who passes the ancient church
> Stops in the shade of its belfry-porch,
> And ponders the wonderful life of him
> Who lies at rest in that charnel dim.
> Long shall the traveller strain his eye
> From the railroad car, as it plunges by,
> And the vanishing town behind him search
> For the slender spire of the Whitefield Church,
> And feel for one moment the ghosts of trade,
> And fashion, and folly, and pleasure laid,
> By the thought of that life of pure intent,
> That voice of warning yet eloquent,
> Of one on the errands of angels sent.
> And if where he labored the flood of sin
> Like a tide from the harbor-bar sets in,
> And over a life of time and sense
> The church-spires lift their vain defence,
> As if to scatter the bolts of God
> With the points of Calvin's thunder-rod, —
> Still, as the gem of its civic crown,
> Precious beyond the world's renown,
> His memory hallows the ancient town!"

XIV.

THE MUSE OF CHORAL SONG.

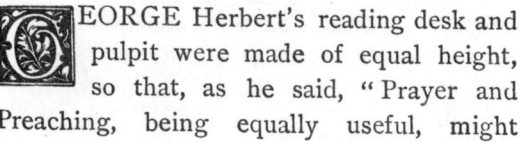

GEORGE Herbert's reading desk and pulpit were made of equal height, so that, as he said, "Prayer and Preaching, being equally useful, might agree like brethren and have an equal honor." These two were esteemed as the essential parts of divine worship in the colonial meeting-house; the service was called "The publick ordinances of praying and preaching." Singing was not specified as a part of the service, although it was practiced, and so badly practiced that the "speaking contemptuously of singing psalms" was notorious.

A treatise, called "Singing of Psalms a Gospel Ordinance," was published by John Cotton, of Boston, in the year 1647. The necessity for such a publication seems to imply that psalm-singing was not a general custom in the meeting-houses. After all that was printed on the subject, there was, in the first century of New England, nothing that could be called a service of song; no harmonious band of singers "to make one sound to be heard in praising and thanking the Lord, saying: 'For he is good; for his mercy endureth forever.'" The Bay Psalm Book, "imprinted 1640," which was used in some parts of New England, was prepared by three ministers, neither of whom had a strand of music or poetry in his soul. It asks us to sing:—

> "Lift up thy foot on hye,
> Unto the desolations
> of perpetuity:
> Thy foe within the Sanctuary
> hath done all lewd designs.
> Amid the Church thy foes doe roare:
> their Banners set for signes."

The best specimen of versification in the book is "Psalme 137." Yet it must have bewildered the rustics who launched themselves "The rivers on of Babilon," to learn where they were going to land:—

> "The rivers on of Babilon
> there when wee did sit downe:
> Yea even then wee mourned, when
> wee remembered Sion.

> Our harps wee did hang it amid,
>   upon the willow tree.
> Because there they that us away
>   led in captivitee,
> Requir'd of us a song, thus
>   askt mirth: us waste who laid,
> Sing us among a Sions song,
>   unto us then they said."

A much needed apology appears in the preface of this book, which reassures the stumbling singer in these words: "If the Verses are not alwayes so smooth and elegant as some may desire or expect let them consider that God's altar needs not our pollishings. Exodus, 20."

Other hymn books known in New England were Ainsworth's "Book of Psalms englished both in prose and metre," printed at Amsterdam in the year 1612. Older than this was the Sternhold and Hopkins hymnody which, during the reign of Queen Elizabeth, had been "permitted rather than allowed" in the Church of England; it was bound in the covers of the Book of Common Prayer, and was rated as a work of superior excellence until the hymnal of Tate and Brady appeared in the year 1696. Then came hymns composed by Isaac Watts, which, in the course of time, crowded out all others. Up to the year 1781, forty editions of his psalms and hymns had been published in New England. The author was a non-conformist theologian, and a preacher to the Mark Lane congregation in London. His religious opinions were more liberal than those of his times; he did not scowl at all Sunday recreations; he said, in one of his hymns, —

> "Religion never was design'd
> To make our pleasures less."

He rejected Calvin's doctrine that a certain number of the human race have been predestined, as reprobates, to condemnation and punishment; he imagined heaven to be the culmination of all good tastes and habits formed on earth. His hymns, coming to the cheerless and shivering services of worship in the colonial meeting-house, were like the coming of a bright and hopeful guest to a disconsolate fireside. Some of them have been acknowledged to be the hymns of a true poet; and these are still said to be more suitable for the service of divine worship than those of any other English composer. Who has forgotten the hymns of Dr. Watts that were sung in the meeting-house of his childhood?

> "When I survey the wondrous cross
>   On which the Prince of Glory died,
> My richest gain I count but loss,
>   And pour contempt on all my pride."

Or this : —

> "There is a land of pure delight,
>   Where saints immortal reign,
> Infinite day excludes the night,
>   And pleasures banish pain."

Or this : —

> "Joy to the world! the Lord is come :
>   Let earth receive her King;
> Let every heart prepare Him room,
>   And heaven and nature sing."

Or this : —

> "Jesus shall reign where'er the sun
>   Does his successive journeys run;
> His kingdom stretch from shore to shore,
>   Till moons shall wax and wane no more."

It may be said that Watts has written the songs of the church. For nearly two centuries his lyric poems have been sung, and are sung to-day wherever the English language is spoken. The reason for this must be that no other poet has so well expressed the devotional spirit, or has so closely sympathized with the experiences of a religious life.

Are you penitent? There is the hymn: —

"Show pity, Lord! O Lord, forgive;
Let a repenting rebel live;
Are not Thy mercies large and free?
May not a sinner trust in Thee?"

Are you truthful? There is the hymn: —

"Thus far the Lord hath led me on;
Thus far His power prolongs my days:
And every evening shall make known
Some fresh memorials of His grace."

Are you desirous of rendering a tribute of homage to the Divine Being? There is the hymn: —

"From all that dwell below the skies,
Let the Creator's praise arise;
Let the Redeemer's name be sung
Thro' every land, by every tongue."

And yet when the hymns of Dr. Watts appeared, many theologians of New England who had been laboriously singing from the Bay Psalm Book, or from the Sternhold and Hopkins version, stood still, not knowing, as they said, what hymns of Dr. Watts should be sung as sacred, and what should be sung as profane. Some of them thought that carnal men should not sing at all. In the year

1736, ministers of Boston were discussing and doubting the propriety of singing any "hymns of mere human composure," and they objected to singing those which were not paraphrases of the Psalms of David.

There appears to have been no scientific knowledge of music in New England until the early part of the last century. It is said that but five or six tunes were in use, and the only identity which these had, as used in different towns, was in the names. St. Mary's sung in Boston was a different St. Mary's from that which vibrated harshly in the meeting-houses on the banks of the Connecticut River; and neither of them resembled that which frightened the babes in "ye Government of New Haven with ye Plantations in combination therewith." All tunes were like traditions handed down by ear, and so changed were they in the transmission that their original form was lost. In Old England the tunes had been left to the mercy of every parish clerk. Records of archdeacons' courts show that the clerk was punished for singing the psalms in church service "with such a jesticulous tone and altitonant voyce, viz. squeaking like a pigg which doth not only interrupt the other voyces but is altogether dissonant and disagreeing unto any musicall harmonie."

A letter printed in "The Spectator," at London, October 25, 1711, tells us how psalm-singing produced discords in the congregations of old England: —

"Sir; — I am a country clergyman, and, hope you will lend me your assistance in ridiculing some little indecencies which cannot so properly be exposed from the pulpit.

"A widow lady who straggled this summer from London into my parish for the benefit of the air, as she says, appears every Sunday at church with many fashionable extravagancies, to the great astonishment of my congregation.

"But what gives us most offense is her theatrical manner of singing the psalms. She introduces about fifty Italian airs into the hundredth psalm; and whilst we begin 'All people' in the old solemn tune of our forefathers, she in a quite different key runs divisions on the vowels and adorns them with the graces of Nicolini. If she meets with an 'eke,' or 'aye,' which are frequent in the metre of Hopkins and Sternhold, we are certain to hear her quavering them half a minute after us to some sprightly airs of the opera. I know her principles and that she will plead toleration, which allows her non-conformity in this particular; but I beg you to acquaint her that singing of psalms in a different tune from the rest of the congregation is a sort of schism not tolerated by that act."

The first efforts to teach a choir to sing "by rule" instead of "by rote," in the colonial meeting-house, were opposed as opening a door to popery; it being declared by some of the old-fashioned singers that "fa, sol, la" was the voice of the Pope in disguise. Each party accused the other of disturbing public worship; the opponents of the new way of singing claimed that the old way was more solemn, and that the new way was wrong because young people readily fell into it. "Last week," says the "New England Courant" of September 16, 1723, "a Council of Churches was held at the South Part of Brantrey to regulate the Disorders occasioned by Regular Singing in that place, Mr. Niles the minister having suspended seven or eight of the Church for persisting in their Singing by Rule contrary (as he apprehended) to the result of a former Council; but by this Council the suspended Brethren are restored to Communion, their suspension declared unjust, and the Congregation ordered to sing by Rote and Rule alternately for the satisfaction of both parties."

Some congregations did not understand the merits of the controversy well enough to have any opinion about it. I find on the Stamford records the following amiable decision, dated "geneway ye 28, 1747 — Voted. y^t Mr. Jona Bell, or any other man agreed upon to sing or tune ye salm in his absence in times of publickt worship may tune it in ye old way or new way, which suits you best." The new way of singing did suit them best in many meeting-houses; and it gradually broke up the custom of reading aloud the hymns, line by line, to the singers, — a custom first introduced at Plymouth for the benefit of worshipers who could not read. This custom prevailed in all parts of New England for a long period, because it removed, as is stated in Lincoln's "History of Worcester," "the embarrassment resulting from the ignorance of those who were more skillful in giving sound to notes, than in deciphering letters."

The fierceness of the controversy caused by the change in methods of psalm-singing may be seen in a petition sent by Joseph Hawley, of Farmington, to the legislature at Hartford, in May, 1725, which

"humbly sheweth" that "Deacon hart ye Chorister one Sabbath day In setting ye psalm attempted to sing Bella tune — and your memorialist being used to ye old way supposed ye deacon had aimed at Cambridge short tune and set it wrong, whereupon your petitioner Raised his Voice in ye sd short tune and ye people followed him, & so there was an unhappy Discord in ye Singing, and ye Blame was all imputed to your poor petitioner, and John Hooker Esq[r] sent for him & fined him for breach of Sabbath, and so your poor petitioner is Layed under a very heavie Scandal & Reproach & Rendered vile & prophane fir what he did in ye fear of God."

Palfrey, in his centennial discourse at Barnstable, quotes from the town records that the peace of the parish was invaded in the year 1726 by a quarrel about the new style of singing, and the civil power was called upon "to detect and bear testimony against such iniquity." The ancient town of Windsor, in Connecticut, did not regard the new fashion as an iniquity; for there it was admitted to an equal footing with the old fashion by a decision to sing "in the old way" in the morning and "in the new way" in the afternoon. Duxbury voted, in the year 1780, that the psalms should "be sung without being read line by line." At Worcester, about the same time, it was voted "that the mode of singing be without reading the psalms line by line." Such is the tenacity of life in religious customs that, on the next Sunday, when a hymn had been announced by the minister, Deacon Chamberlain, determined to follow the custom of his life, arose and read aloud the first line as he had always done. The singers, whose bold array stretched along the front of the gallery, sang the first line, and immediately passed on to the second line, without pausing for the deacon; while he, with all the strength of his voice, read the lines one after another, and so continued to read until the progress of the choir overpowered him. Then he left the meeting-house, mortified and weeping. But the church, not satisfied with this triumph over the venerable man, publicly censured him and deprived him of communion, because he had absented himself "from the public ordinances on the Lord's Day."

The jiggery muse of choral song was not contented with upsetting the musical practices in New England meeting-houses; she skipped over the border and shocked, by her antics, English congregations in Canada and Nova Scotia. In the year 1770, she entered St. Paul's, the Episcopal meeting-house at Halifax, where she caused the organist "to indulge in artistic Musick too freely;" so that, as was written at the time, "the Major part of the Congregation do not understand the Words or the Musick and cannot join in them." The vestry met, and ordered that thereafter the organist shall play only " such Tunes as are solemn, and that he Play the Psalm Tunes in a Familiar manner without unnecessary Graces." There may have been something the matter with the organ; for tradition says that a Spanish ship was brought into Halifax as a prize, and in her cargo was found the organ on its way to a Roman Catholic chapel in the West Indies. It was removed from the prize ship to the choir of St. Paul's, where it practiced those "unnecessary Graces" which offended the congregation.

XV.

THE BIBLE AND THE CONFESSIONAL.

IN the year 1541, "Payed for a Byble for ye towns part, four shillings." So runs an item in the churchwarden's accounts of the parish of North Elmham in Old England. Two years previous, the Bible had been printed at London, in folio size, under the direction of Coverdale and the patronage of Cranmer. Another edition appeared in the year 1540, for which Cranmer wrote a preface teaching that "Scripture should be read of the lay and vulgar people;" and in the same year a royal proclamation required every parish in England to procure, for public use, a Bible of the largest size, under penalty of forty shillings monthly for a delay. This Bible was to be set up in the churches where it might be read by the people, although it was not as yet used in the public services of worship.

There was no Bible set up in the colonial meeting-house to "be read of the lay and vulgar people;" nor was there any reading from the Bible by the minister in the pulpit during the first century of New England. When the Brattle Street meeting-house was erected at Boston, the society formed to worship in it, which included many of the best families living in the town, startled the orthodox community by proposing several innovations upon the church customs of the times. The chief of these were that the minister should read from the Bible to the congregation; that baptism should be administered to parents and children on lighter terms than a personal profession of religion; that the public confession of sins by communicants should be abolished; that the right to vote for election of a minister should not be confined alone to men. These plans were set forth in a "Manifesto or Declaration," which attracted so much attention that the church was called, in ridicule, the manifesto church.

In regard to a public reading of the Bible, its declaration was: "We design only the true and pure Worship of God, according to the Rules appearing plainly to us in His Word. ... We judge it therefore most suitable and convenient, that in our Publick Worship some part of the Holy Scripture be read by the Minister at his discretion." As to public confessions, it said: "We assume not to our selves to impose upon any a Publick Relation of their Experiences; however if any one think himself bound in Conscience to make such a Relation, let him do it." And the letter of the society inviting Benjamin Coleman to come the seas over and be their minister said: "We propose that the Holy Scripture be publicly read every Sabbath in the Worship of God which is not practiced in the other Churches of New England at the present time, and that we may lay aside the Relation of Experiences which are imposed in other Churches in order to the admission of persons to the Lord's Table."

The manifesto called forth impertinent rebukes from the leading ministers of Boston and its vicinity, including one from that minister at Salem who had excommunicated Rebecca Nourse. When the news reached Cotton Mather, minister in the North meet-

ing-house, he goes to his diary and writes:
"A company of headstrong men in the town,
the chief of whom are full of malignity to
the holy ways of our churches, have built
in the town another meeting-house. And
without the advice or knowledge of the ministers in the vicinity they have published
under the title of a Manifesto, certain articles that utterly subvert our churches."

The churches which this diarist represented stood on a very insecure foundation,
if they were to be turned bottom side up
by the declaration that the Holy Scriptures
should be read in the services of public
worship, and that the disgraceful confessional
should be abolished! His malignity is kept
at the boiling point for four or five months,
when it runs over into his diary again. He
writes, using capital letters more profusely
than usual: "I see Satan beginning a terrible Shake unto the Churches of New England and the Innovators that have sett up a
New Church in Boston (a New one indeed!)
have made a Day of Temptation among us.
The men are Ignorant, Arrogant, Obstinate
and full of malice and slander, and they fill
the Land with Lyes, in the misrepresenta-

tions thereof I am a very singular sufferer. Wherefore I set apart this day again for prayer in my study to cry mightily unto God."

How different was the spirit of this man, whose habit it was "to cry mightily unto God" whenever the course of events did not suit his purposes, from that of Samuel Sewall; who, after receiving a visit from the minister of the new church, wrote in his diary: "I told him If God should please by them to hold forth any Light that had not been seen or entertained before, I should be so far from envying it that I should rejoice in it."

Reading the Holy Scriptures as part of the services of public worship was a novelty that won its way to favor slowly. It was not until the year 1737 that the Old South Church of Boston voted that they "be read in Public after the first Prayer in the morning and Afternoon." Medford town voted, in the year 1759, "to read the Holy Scriptures in the congregation;" Duxbury voted, in the year 1790, that they "should be read every Lord's day by the minister;" and at Framingham, in the year 1792, the Scriptures were ordered "to be read in public on the Sabbath, and a Bible procured for that purpose."

Some editions of the Bible which were to be obtained in colonial times had not been published by approved authority; as an edition of the year 1653, which represented St. Paul as saying: "Know ye not that the unrighteous shall inherit the Kingdom of Heaven?" Other editions were spotted by translator's and printer's errors. The most notorious of these was an edition published in the year 1631, by Robert Barker, a London printer enjoying the highest favor of King Charles the First; in which the negative was omitted from the Seventh Commandment. A formal complaint was made against the printer by Archbishop Laud before that rigorous body of censors known as The Star Chamber, and by them the edition of one thousand copies was condemned to be burned in public; Barker and his associate, Martin Lucas, were fined three hundred pounds each, and were locked in prison for one year. But all the copies were not burned. One appeared in the book market in the year 1855, which was examined by the Society of Antiquaries in London and was then called the "Wicked Bible," as their records say, "from the circumstance of its being filled with gross and scandalous typographical errors not the least remarkable of which is the omission of the important word 'not' in the Seventh Commandment." Other copies have been found, imperfect by missing leaves; and there are known to be six perfect copies of the "Wicked Bible" now in existence. One of these, which fell into my hands, has three religious publications bound with it. The first is a catechism of eighty-six pages on the doctrines of the Bible, having this quaint title: "The Way to trve happines leading to the Gate of knovvledge;" the second is The Book of Common Prayer; the third publication is "The Whole Book of Psalmes Collected into English Meeter by Thomas Sternhold, John Hopkins, and others, conferred with the Hebrew, with apt notes to sing them withall. London, 1616." In a blank space on a page of the catechism I found these words, written distinctly in an ink which had become brown with age: —

> "ffrancis Chamberling
> her Book god give her
> grais on It to Look."

And, whether she lived in New England or in Old England, it is to be hoped that she received a full measure of the grace which she needed when she studied the commandments, and for which she so modestly asked more than two hundred years ago.

The public confession, commonly called the relation of experiences, was a custom brought from Old England; it appeared in the first church organized by John Winthrop's company in New England, and it continued to be a custom of the churches for two hundred years. The sinner made confession before the whole congregation. When it was propounded to the Old South Church of Boston, in the year 1717, "whether Captain Nathaniel Oliver's Confession should be before the Church or before the Congregation," Judge Sewall said: "I opposed the former as not agreeing with the universal practice. Not fit that the penitent should prescribe before what auditory his confession should be." Authority for this custom was claimed to rest in certain verses of the eighteenth chapter of the Gospel by St. Matthew; it ignored the responsibility of an individual for his sins, making the church responsible for them, and it assumed that the minister and the church as a body had the power to forgive them by restoring the sinner to fellowship, on his making a penitent confession of his sinful acts. The style of preaching tended to keep alive the confessional. Those were days when fear ruled the common mind. Fear of eternal perdition caused skeletons, that were locked up in the cupboard of conscience, to stir and rattle, and to come out and stand up in the great alley of the meeting-house, where confessions were made of sins which, even in the time of the Apostle Paul, were not to be named publicly. The repentance of the penitents was, to quote the maxim of La Rochefoucauld, "not so much a regret for the ill we have done, as a fear of the ill that may come to us in consequence of our doing."

With the Presbyterians of Scotland, in the seventeenth century, church discipline was more severe than it was with the Congregationalists of New England. The Scotch minister could put his sinning parishioners in the town stocks; he could compel them to stand up during the entire service, as a schoolmaster orders naughty children to stand up until the school is dismissed. The penitents, clad in linen robes and standing in the alley of the meeting-house, were doomed not only to hear their sins denounced from the pulpit, but also to pay a fine for the sinning.[1]

The reverend Mr. Huntington, when pleading against the inquisitive forms of church discipline before an ecclesiastical council sitting in the meeting-house at Stockbridge, Massachusetts, said: "My impleaders claim that the church have that right committed to them. But where do they find it? Not in the word of God; not in the reason and nature of things. Nor is it possible, gentlemen, that the church should be able to judge in such cases with any propriety. Persons many times have a clear, decisive reason why

[1] Waddell, *History of Auldhame, Tyninghame, and Whitekirk in East Lothian.*

It is recorded in the Acts of the Privy Council, of the year 1554, that "Robert Wendham of the parish of St. Giles in the Field, tailor, for shaving a dog was appointed to repair on Sunday next to the parish church and there openly confess his folly, according to the order prescribed."

they should marry each other, and they know it is their duty to do so; and yet it is a very unlawful, wicked thing for them to make their reasons public by communicating them to a whole church. Many church members — I speak it with great detestation — have laid themselves under clear, inviolable obligation to marry, by means of an antecedent criminal commerce, which never ought to be known to the world, and never can be unless they tell of it. A man has no right to publish his own sins; his duty is to confess them to God and forsake them."

It may be said that there was then more identity between the minister and his people than there is now. In colonial times his position and influence were strengthened by what was called "the communion of the churches," on which he could lean, and by the power of church discipline of which he was the dispenser for harm as well as for good. Let me give an example of the harm. In the year 1723, at Durham, New Hampshire, James Davis and his wife, being about to join the church, their former minister, who had been dismissed in a quarrel, sent a protest against their admission, " by virtue of ye communion of churches." By such virtue he stigmatized Davis as a "sacrilegious fraud;" he called him and his wife "unbaptised heathen man and woman." Here is a part of what he wrote to their minister in Durham:—

"Rev^{end} Hon. & beloved

"Understanding Col Davis & his wife are ab^t to Joyn in full communion with your church this is by virtue of ye communion of churches to enter my objection against them for scandalous crimes, untill their publick confession & reformation.

"1st crime against him is his hipocrisy in pretending he could not unite with our church on acc^{tt} of Capt Jones who (as he said) had taken a false oath.

"2^d crime is his Sacrilegious fraud in his being The ringleader of the peoples rase of my first years sallary— retaining 16 pounds thereof now almost sixteen years.

"3^d crime is his Sacrilegious covetousness of the parsonage land for his son Daniel, acting thereby like Ahab coveting & forceable entry upon Naboths Vineyard.

"Besides his the s^d Jas Davis being so desperately & notoriously wise in his own conceit his pretending to have so much religious discourse in his mouth & yet live so long (40 years) in hatred unto contempt of & stand neuter from our crucified Saviour."

We may not believe that there were many ministers of this stripe in the rural parishes of New England. And yet, as late as the year 1777, Stephen West, minister at Stockbridge, used the whip of church discipline in a manner that was suited to the temper of religionists in the Middle Ages. This is the story: John Fisk, who had been an officer in the military service, was employed to keep a school, in the vicinity of which lived Mrs. Levina Deane, a young widow of an amiable character and a member of the church. Mr. Fisk prevailed with Mrs. Deane to take him into her house as a boarder, where he performed the religious exercises of the family, morning and evening and at table, as a religious and gifted man. And being a gentleman of fine address he was attentive to recommend himself to the favor of Mrs. Deane; and was successful. The church, being apprised that there was a purpose of marriage between them, warned Mrs. Deane, on motion of the minister, against proceeding; inasmuch as they judged that Mr. Fisk, not being a member of the church, was "an immoral and profane person." Mrs. Deane, finding that the marriage would be offensive to the church, made all efforts in her power to conquer her passion for Mr. Fisk, but was unable to do so. They were married, and she was excommunicated by vote of the church, which the minister formulated in these words: "That Levina Fisk be excluded from the communion of this church till she manifest a sense of her wickedness in marrying to Mr. Fisk, and repentance of it."

Was her "repentance of it" to be a divorce? She called for an ecclesiastical council, and West allowed her to have one on condition that he select its members. He summoned eleven ministers from parishes in Massachusetts and Connecticut, who sat with him in the meeting-house, and deliberated on the matter, and approved the excommunication of Mrs. Fisk. This act of persecution by ecclesiastics of the established church of New England reminds me of an incident described in the "Ingoldsby Legends:" the great Lord Cardinal had lost a valuable turquoise ring; he summoned into his presence all the clergy, the monks, and nuns connected with his establishment, and before them he solemnly pronounced a series of tremendous cursing.

> "Never was heard such a terrible curse;
> But what gave rise
> To no little surprise,
> Nobody seemed one penny the worse."

XVI.

THE HOUR-GLASS.

"Turning the accomplishments of many years
Into an hour-glass."
Henry V.

THE hour-glass ended the services in the colonial meeting-house. It was an inheritance from Old England, where it was to be seen in every parish church; and that it might be distinctly seen, a candle was burning behind it whose light passed through the running sands. "Payd to the Smithe for mendinge the houreglas Candlesticke 2*d*.," say the records of St. Mary's in Reading of the year 1603. It was necessary to renew the hour-glass frequently, for accidents made brief its life. In the year 1570, the churchwardens of the parish of St. Matthew, in London, "paide for an ower glasse 4*d*.;" and in the year 1579 they "paide for a nowere glasse 3*d*.;" and in the year 1584, they "paide for an owar glasse 12*d*." At that time the glass stood, not on the pulpit, but on a bracket, or a frame; or it was hung on a wall facing the congregation. In the churchwarden's accounts of St. Mary's, Lambeth, of the year 1579, is written: " Payde for the frame on which the hower standeth, 1*s.* 4*d.*;" and in the accounts of St. Mary's, Shrewsbury, of the year 1597, is a charge "for makeinge a thing for the hower glasse, 9*d.*"

The purpose of the hour-glass is stated in the parish records of St. Katherine's, Aldgate, London; wherein is mentioned a payment for "one hour-glass hanging by the pulpit where the preacher doth make his sermon that he may know how the hour passeth." A legend sometimes engraved on the bands that held it in place said:—

"As this sand runneth
So your life fadeth."

Sometimes the legend was in Latin; as, "Pereunt et imputantus," which is to be translated as expressing a thought of the preacher, "I am accountable for the hours that perish under my sermon." As the hour-glass was a measure of the time, and a sign of its passing, a suitable inscription would have been that which was given to the sun-dial : —

"I marke the Time! Saye, Gossip, dost thou soe?"

The gossips did mark it; they watched the hour-glass, not because they enjoyed a right godly admonition of an hour's length any more than people do now; but they must see that they were getting all the preaching that they were paying for. That the long sermons of those colonial days — in the forenoon and in the afternoon of every Sunday — were wearisome to the hearers is shown by the methods in vogue to keep men and women awake and wretched boys quiet, and by the eagerness of all to get out of doors as soon as the sermon was ended.

It was indeed a severe exercise to listen to hour-glass sermons in which the mysteries of fixed fate, free will, foreknowledge absolute, were expounded. The preacher told the story of Adam's transgression; and how all mankind, sinning with him, fell with him, and rested thenceforth under the wrath of God; —

"And how, of His will and pleasure,
　All souls, save a chosen few,
Were doomed to the quenchless burning,
　And held in the way thereto."

As if to make the sermon more attractive to the listeners, it was sometimes aimed at one or two conspicuous families in the congregation. These were held up by name; and exhortations, applications, and conclusions were ejected at them from the pulpit, firstly to the husband, secondly to the wife, thirdly to the children. Meanwhile curiosity was craning its neck in all parts of the meeting-house to get a sight of the culprits, until the hour-glass sands had run down.

As the preacher became a man of much importance during the Puritan period of English history, a sermon of two hours' length was sometimes inflicted upon a congregation; and with an air of authority not to be disputed the preacher turned the hour-glass for a second run of the sands of time. A story is told of an incident at Hadleigh, in Old England, where an independent lecturer had taken the place of an ejected vicar. The lecturer had got through the first glass of his sermon and half through the second glass, when, showing no signs of being on the home-stretch, the audience one by one began to creep out. Suddenly, in a pause of the discourse, the old parish clerk arose, and said: "Honored Sir! When your reverence hath finished, be pleased to close the church and put the key under the door." And he went out also.

A preacher of eccentric manners was Hugh Peters, of Salem; he was also a politician. He went to England and became chaplain to Cromwell, and a regicide, for which occupations he was beheaded at London in the year 1660. In those days people spelled their names as the fancy took them; they had no rule to go by; nothing beyond an approximation of the sound of a name as spoken was regarded when writing it. When this minister wrote himself as Hu Peter, he probably rejoiced in this orthographical license. A painting represents him in the pulpit reversing an hour-glass and saying to the congregation: "I know you are good fellows; stay and take another glass!" This anecdote was rated so well, that it was sent over the ocean and given to several preachers.

One of these was Daniel Burgess, who was preaching to Londoners against the sin of drunkenness. The sands of the hour-glass had run down. "Brethren," said he, "of this damnable sin of drinking there is more to be said; nay, much more; let us have another glass!"

The preacher with his hour-glass had his own way in the colonial meeting-house. He could go on forever and then begin again; and when he came to "finally, lastly, and to conclude," he might be a long way from the end, even if the hour-glass had stopped its running sands. At Boston, one day, John Winthrop went to hear Mr. Hooker preach. The fame of the preacher was great in the little community, and therefore the governor must go to hear him. In one of his letters he tells what occurred. The preacher, he says, "having gone on with much strength of voice and intention of spirit about a quarter of an hour, he was at a stand, and told the people that God had deprived him both of his strength and matter, etc., and so went forth." This probably means that he started so vehemently that he forgot what he was preaching about, and broke down, and went out of the meeting-house to recover himself. Not recognizing the purpose for which he had been divinely "deprived both of his strength and matter," he did not stay out, but came back to the pulpit after an absence of half an hour; as Winthrop tells it, the preacher "about half an hour after returned again and went on to very good purpose about two hours!"

Here were two hours and a quarter of sermonizing with an interval of half an hour of cold silence. Did the governor and the congregation fall asleep in that interval? If not, they neglected an opportunity which had been mercifully put in their way. The incident, as Winthrop relates it, indicates that the preacher felt himself to be put on show, and that the audience desired to see the show to its end.

"If I had my time to live over again," said Martin Luther, "my sermons would be shorter. I would not have preachers torment their hearers with long and tedious preaching." Perhaps the colonial preacher would say the same words, could he reappear and summon before him the men and women to whom he preached "while the years and the hours were." The hour-glass that stands on the pulpit in Hogarth's picture has the legend, "Omnia fumus erunt," — they all are dust. And the colonial preacher, he, too, is

> — "dead and gone;
> You can see his leaning slate
> In the graveyard, and thereon
> Read his name and date."